What Others Are Saying

Pastor Scott was a tremendous support during my struggles with anxiety and depression. Sharing from his own experience of depression and anxiety, he made me feel like he could relate to my suffering. I could be open and honest about my past without feeling I was being judged. He has godly wisdom that I trusted and followed. He encouraged me, and I had great confidence in his counsel. He helped me to see some things that were very fearful to me in a new light. I knew that he cared, and I was touched by the way he remembered me in prayer. He is kind, and he is as real as it gets! I thank God for him in my life.

—Bernadette H.
Bayshore, New York

Pastor Scott has been a huge blessing to me. The Lord sent him into my life six years ago in my darkest hour, and he has been a major contributor to my recovery from depression, anxiety, and cutting issues. I know that Pastor Scott loves the Lord with all his heart, and he does his best to follow God's lead in any given situation. His wisdom comes from experience, and he has a passion for helping others in their times of need, to direct them to the Lord in all circumstances. I truly believe that if God hadn't sent Pastor Scott and his church into my life when He did, I would not be here to write this. I praise the Lord for His perfect timing and for a man willing to listen to God's heart in helping to heal His children.

—Jena M. P.
Rochester, New Hampshire

Pastor Scott is truly a blessing to have in my life. He has helped me in so many ways over the years with depression, anxiety, and self-esteem issues. When I am with him, I know that he is completely listening to me and that he wants to help as much as he can. He prays with me, comforts me, and really allows me to feel and talk through things. He makes me feel like he cares, as if I were his own daughter, and that means so much. His faith is contagious, and it is what makes him such an amazing counselor. God surely speaks through him. He reminds me that I am a child of God and that I am worth so much. I only hope that everyone could have someone like Pastor Scott in their life, to selflessly listen, pray for, and speak the truth of Jesus through his counseling. I am truly blessed God has placed him in my life!

—Nichole R.
New York

I think my anxiety started when I was in first grade. I went to Catholic school in the late sixties, and I was terrified of the nuns. I was always afraid of doing something wrong.

Depression started in my teens. I remember the words of a poem I wrote for a high school English class.

Who am I, I want to die.
I'm lonely and confused.
Days go by, I wonder why.
I'm tortured and abused.

I had a good family. I was not tortured or abused by them, or the nuns in Catholic school. But for some reason, I carried this depression and anxiety around with me. It has drained all my energy, made me isolate myself, not wanting to go anywhere, or do anything, or see anyone, unable to enjoy anything or know how to have fun. I have said to myself, "I wish I was dead" and "I wish I was never born." I have had times when the depression was only mild, and times of complete terror, a cold chill in the pit of my chest, followed by complete emptiness. It has debilitated me to the point of staying in bed for days at a time.

I have been on antidepressants with some relief, but the feelings always seem to return. I remember getting in my car, or driving, and hoping I would have a fatal car crash. I remember being jealous of people with cancer and then the guilt I felt (I am an oncology nurse). I have sat in my car in the garage with the motor running…but I always went back in the house. I was afraid I would go to hell for killing myself.

I came to Christ about seven years ago. Yes, I am definitely a new creation, not the person I used to be. My entire mindset is different. But I still get depressed and anxious. I have counseled with Pastor Scott. He is very open about his experience with severe depression and anxiety, almost took his life. I knew he understood what I felt. We would talk and pray together. I would text him often in the early mornings (always the worst time for me). He always told me it would get better, and it did. But most of all he assured me that all of my anxieties and depression had a purpose. That God loves me, and knows what I am going through, that I needed to experience this in order to have a closer personal relationship with God. That this "weakness" kept me in constant touch with God, and that would help me to help others who suffer in the same way. Knowing that God is in control of all things, at all times, and trusting Him is what I needed to learn. It lifted a huge burden off me – trying to figure out how to fix this or live with this on my own.

I still have bouts of anxiety and depression. I take medications that help. But through prayer, and trusting in Christ, I have been able to stop it before it becomes debilitating. Through constant prayer, I ask God to keep me from the darkness of depression and the paralyzing anxiety. God hears and answers prayer, through Christ Jesus. I will never stop praying. He will never let me down. I will use my experience to help others whenever I can.

—Laura H.
Middle Island, New York

Depression, Anxiety, and the Child of God

Depression, Anxiety, and the Child of God
Part 1

WHAT IN THE WORLD IS GOING ON?
ISAIAH 49:13

SCOTT R. KRANIAK

YorkshirePublishing
www.yorkshirepublishing.com
Write Now.

ISBN: 978-1-947247-23-9
Depression, Anxiety, and the Child of God
Copyright © 2015 by Scott R. Kraniak

Yorkshire Publishing
3207 South Norwood Avenue
Tulsa, Oklahoma 74135
www.YorkshirePublishing.com
918.394.2665

What in the World Is Going On?
Isaiah 49:13

Can faith, counseling, and even medication
coexist in the church today?

*The silent taboo of mental illness and emotional stress in
the church—let's break the silence once and for all.*

By S. R. Kraniak, ThB-MMCC

Foreword by
Steve Rise, PhD, LCSW-R

Don't forget to look for the companion book called
Depression Anxiety and the Child of God
(The Twelve-Month Devotional)
also by S. R. Kraniak

This book is dedicated to many people

*To all of the silent screams of the lonely people out there who suffer
with the worst kind of agony that no one seems to even want to hear*

*To my wife Julie who held my hand during the darkest
days I can remember, who kept me focused on Christ and
whose unwavering faith in Christ never faltered*

*To my dear friend and associate Steve Reis for hooking me up
and counseling me, and giving me comfort through the comfort he
received while going through his own dark time many years ago*

*To Doctor Z, as we like to call him, a humble and godly psychiatrist
who, besides being a good friend to me, also became an associate in the
battle of saving many lost souls in the grips of depression and anxiety*

My most memorable times were our prayer times together

*And last but not least, to Jesus Christ—the Mighty
Counselor and Everlasting Lord. Thank you for your
grace, patience, and allowing me to go through it one
more time so I would be motivated to write this book*

Good does come from bad and the sun does shine after the storm.

Special Dedication

This book and additional devotional (sold separately) are also dedicated to Jennifer Palagonia born January 13, 1982, and left this world on June 28, 2014.

Jen was a dear young lady which I counseled for many years, yet unfortunately Jen gave up too soon and believed the lies of the destroyer. Jen was a beautiful and brave young lady. Through her passing and at her funeral service many eyes were open to this silent monster called mental illness. So many people were moved to see what they didn't even know existed. Through her death, many are coming to understand and many are seeking God for the first time. As much as a blessing Jen was in her life she is also being so in her passing. I will miss you, Jen, but your story will save countless lives so this never has to happen again.

Acknowledgments

I would like to take this time to thank those
who helped make this book a reality

To my team of editors who spent a good part of a year on their
own time looking over my gibberish and making sense out of it

Lois Dipol
Linda Ziroli
Melodie Rubio

Heather Davis
Artwork and Photography

Lauren Ziroli
Cover Model

My family for allowing me to spend every free hour
writing when I could have been with them
Julie, Jacob, Aaron, and Luke

Jena Pinkum
For all the research and fact-finding you did for this project
plus your constant pats on the back that kept me focused

Dr. Zodiatis, MD
For being the only psychiatrist I know that besides being
a godly man is also a doctor who will pray with you.

I enjoyed our times in prayer and also the blessings of
being able to send my patients to you knowing that
they are in good hands when medication is needed.

Thank you also for helping me when I
was in need of your wisdom.

Jennifer LeClaire, news editor at Charisma magazine,
for her article on depression in the pulpit.

Carlene Hill Byron, for her amazing work on
depression and mental illness in the church

The Minnesota Department of Health
Minnesota Commissioner of Health, Dr. Ed Ehlinger
US Centers for Disease Control and Prevention (CDC)

The Adverse Childhood Experiences
(ACE) study released by MDH

SAVE (Suicide Awareness Voices for Education)
Minnesota Suicide Prevention Planning Task Force
National Strategy for Suicide Prevention
DHS mental health and crisis services,
the TXT4Life initiative, MDH and local
community suicide prevention efforts

Why I Wrote This Book

This book has been a life obsession for me. After over seventeen years of Christian counseling and meeting so many people in the church who were suffering with emotional issues, I found it disturbing that the church offered little to no help in this area. Sure you could go to your pastor for counseling, but most pastors and clergy are not trained in clinical depression and anxiety disorder. What's worse is the stigma placed on Christians who suffered with these ailments. Too many times I have heard these statements by Christian leaders and laypeople alike: *Christians shouldn't be dealing with depression and anxiety, and if you are, it's probably a spiritual issue that can only be fought off with prayer and faith.* Many Christians would come to see me feeling like second-class believers, or even worse, doubting their own salvation. As to medication, the Christian church for the most part is completely opposed to any use of these aids, and to choose to take such mediation was a sure sign that your faith has been abandoned. Even my own circle of friends and associates in the Christian world have opposed my stand on how to handle these heavy emotional issues. I have seen too many people suffering when it was not necessary. Too many Christians looked down upon and shamed to say what they were really struggling with. As in my book on sexual addiction in Christian men, the same stigma was found. "I'm a Christian so addiction to pornography should not be an issue." That is why I wrote my first book (*Spiritual Living in a Sexual World*), exposing myself and my struggles, and if I was the only Christian man out there with these issues, then so be it, but if one man was struggling alone, then he deserved a voice in the wilderness. As to depression and anxiety, the lone voice in the wilderness was even more hidden and banished. It seems that it's a silent cry, one that you are not allowed to have. Funny, as I thought that you can be taking medication for high blood pressure, or for cholesterol, or any other bodily issue and no one would ever bat an eye, but mention emotional issues and medication for them and you were shunned and called faithless. I discovered that emotional pain was the worst kind of pain as no one could see it, there was no bandage you could wear over it, and no one felt compassion for it. Instead you were looked upon as being less of a Christian than you should be. Sin was the only answer, and if you only had faith and were anointed with enough oil, and read enough Scripture and read enough Bible, you should be made whole. Sure some were, but not all. Today 70 percent of the people you sit next to in church are on some type of medication for some emotional issue, yet those 70 percent will never tell you in fear of being blacklisted. I also found that people had very little patience for our emotional breakdowns. They would come over, pray over you, dump five gallons of anointing oil on your head, and claim the demons were gone. If you weren't healed in a few weeks, then people just assumed you were just faking it so you didn't have to work. Or that you just wanted sympathy from the world or an excuse not to participate in life. The ignorance I found in the church was too much to bear, and often it forced many Christians to seek secular counseling who often had much more compassion for them but had no understanding of spiritual things. When I went through my times of dark depression and anxiety, I sought many counselors and found very few versed in the true Christian art. I decided that day to become a true Christian counselor that would deal with these issues the way no one else was dealing with them. I became proficient in Nouthetic counseling or counseling by and through the Word of God yet without being afraid to use some secular avenues also.

I then joined forces with a Christian therapist and a godly man who was a state licensed psychiatrist. Together we formed a trinity of counseling using all facets of our trades, Bible counseling, Christian therapy, and if needed, limited medications. Together we achieved great results often in a tag-team match type setup of coordinated communications over one person. Today I counsel more people with depression and anxiety than anything else. It is an epidemic in the church simply because it is pushed under the rug as an embarrassment. We are losing an entire generation to suicide and depression and debilitating anxiety simply because we cannot understand why faith alone won't heal it. We then conclude if faith cannot heal it, then it must not be real. Again my anger about this ignorance came to a feverous pitch as I saw people being treated for heart attacks and broken legs in secular fashion, yet we didn't offer the same option to those who were suffering with mental issues. If we take an aspirin for a headache, then why not a pill for an emotional issue? If we don't use faith to heal a broken leg, then why is it sacrilege to use secular means to heal a broken mind? Now don't get me wrong, my main focus and goal is *not* to medicate a generation or the church for that matter, but to put all our cards on the table and use which ones are best for each case. In my practice I do not push medication at all and only use it as a last resort if all means tried have been exhausted. Then and only then using my years of experience, I introduce the idea of seeing my psychiatrist associate for medication needs. Certainly having a God-fearing doctor is a plus and one that also is very timid in regard to medication, but if the right one is found, great success can be made. Dear friends, I write this book because in 1997 I fell into a deep clinical depression that didn't have to get that bad, but because of Christian pressures and prejudices, I would not take medication. I simply refused and trusted only in the Lord and faith to heal me. I was prayed over and had what felt like six gallons of anointing oil poured over me. It didn't work and I was dying and I say that in every sense of the word. I could no longer pray, read my Bible, or barely keep food inside me. If it wasn't for my dear sister in California who called me one day and asked me why I didn't try medication, I would be dead. After much arguing, she showed me the logic of taking meds for everything else that ails us, so why shouldn't we take the meds that God has allowed man to invent to also help our misfiring mind to help get the synapses firing again. I was desperate, and so I contacted my family doctor, explained my situation, and after a few attempts at different things, he found the one pill that helped me. No, I wasn't walking around in a drug-induced daze but was able to hear God's Word again, pray, and trust Him, and in time got back on track.

I found out that in my case OCD was the culprit. From there it led me to anxiety, then anxiety attacks, then full-blown depression. Though I never missed a day of work, and never ended up in the hospital, I sure came close. Yet through all of that, I was called to be a pastor, write my first book, and lead many people to Christ and help them with their own emotional disorders. Call me cheating or not trusting God, that's your choice, but what if the greatest faith I exercised was trusting God when He said "This medicine is made for you, why won't you take what I have allowed in this age?" I created penicillin for infection, why can't I use similar things for depression? It was hard as a Christian and for fifteen years I never told a soul I was taking that pill in fear and in pride. I thought to myself, *Why am I so ashamed of this? Why can I take meds for an infection but not for an imbalance in my brain?* Why the stigma, why are so many forced to live a secret and feel less of a Christian than another? I decided back then to stop the madness and speak the truth. Now I don't know what's going on today, but one thing is certain; mental illness and depression is skyrocketing like never before. It is like a plague moving over our land.

Note actor Robin Williams's recent suicide, and we can see that anyone can fall under its curse.

I don't know if it is from the food we eat and all the chemicals we are taking in, or maybe a demonic spiritual attack, but the fact remains we are a generation with so much yet so worried and crippled by fear. Learning about how God wired us can help, but in the meantime we need to get the word out and help first the church, and then once the church is healed, get the word out that Jesus also heals crying minds. So please hear me out, call me crazy or not a child of God, but don't do it until you see if what I say is true or not. Listen, I love the Lord Jesus Christ with all my mind, heart, and soul. I trust Him alone for my salvation, His work alone, and I claim there is no other way to be saved. But I also know what the Lord has taught me and that is, *as Jesus used many ways to heal people in the Bible, He uses many ways to heal us today.* Let us not be so bigoted that we cast out hope when it is just ready to be harvested for healing. I think we all know the story about the man living in a house during a flood warning. He prays to the Lord and says *"Lord, I trust you to save me from this coming flood."* And so the Lord sends him a ranger in a Jeep who says, *"Get in, a flood is coming,"* but the man says, *"No, I am waiting for God to save me, I am trusting in Him by faith."* Then as the water gets past his front door, the sheriff comes by in a rowboat saying, *"Get in, the flood is getting worse"* but again the man says, *"No, I am trusting in Jesus to save me,"* then as the water is above his roof and he is hanging on to his chimney, a helicopter flies over and from the loudspeaker says, *"Grab on to the rope or the flood will kill you,"* but again the man refuses, and as the helicopter flies away and the man is now drowning, he cries out to the Lord and says, *"Lord, I had faith in you, I trusted you, I quoted scripture, I had Deacon John anoint my home with oil, and yet where are you?"* To that the Lord replies,– *"Dear child, I sent you a Jeep, a boat, and a helicopter, and you would not listen or take My help, you only wanted help in the form that you deemed appropriate. Now you are lost and dying."*

Dear friend, I know that's simplistic, but is it really? The Lord has delivered His people throughout the Bible in many ways and through many different people and methods. Sometimes He just healed, but sometimes He parted oceans. Sometimes He did it through the world, and sometimes He asked us to trust Him and obey His command to do a certain thing to find healing. Should we not obey what the Lord is saying today? Please feel free to contact me (depressionanxietygod@gmail.com) or through my blog depressionanxietygod.blogspt.com and give me your story and opinion on this very present people problem today. Maybe I am missing something, or maybe you are.

Note from the Author

This is the first part of this work on depression and anxiety
Make sure to get the companion book called
Depression, Anxiety, and the Child of God
(The Twelve-Month Devotional)

Contents

Foreword

I have known Pastor Scott for several years, and I appreciate his no-frills, direct, and honest approach regarding the brokenness of mankind, the problems inherent to the human condition, and the solutions that are critical to finding healing and restoration. From his own personal experiences, Pastor Scott shares how he suffered the anguish of depression and anxiety, and how these ailments can develop from emotional, physical, mental, or spiritual issues; yet the solution always remains the same—Jesus Christ.

Even though our culture has taught us that pain is bad and must be avoided, Pastor Scott underscores the truth that depression and anxiety, in addition to many other forms of suffering, are to be *embraced* because they serve as teachers that will ultimately create a deeper appreciation of life and a more intimate relationship with the One who created us. Moreover, Pastor Scott emphasizes it is through struggle and suffering that God reveals the amazing plan he has for our lives; for it is only in the Refiner's fire where we learn to find our inherent value, purpose, and identity in Jesus Christ.

—Steve Rise
PhD, LCSW-R

Steve Rise, PhD, LCSW-R, is a board-certified expert in traumatic stress and crisis intervention. He is the founder of New Hope Counseling and the Core Values Model, which employs a multi-modal approach to psychotherapy. Individual, couple, family, group, and corporate counseling services are offered with a specialization in the areas of trauma, stress, anxiety, depressive, and eating disorders and attachment issues throughout one's life span.

Introduction

Depression, anxiety, and *mental illness*—not words you would commonly associate with being a Christian. Medication and psychiatry are also things you would not think a Christian or person of faith would ever have to deal with. Well, I have news for you. Unless you are living on Mars, these are real issues and problems. If it were not so, I would not be writing this book on the issue. I tell you, the lack of understanding that Christians have on this subject really bothers me. From pastors to laypeople, they just don't get it and often point their big self-righteous finger right at us as if we were some subhuman Christian failure. Yes, I have heard it all, as I am sure you have also. Christians shouldn't have depression or anxiety; Christians shouldn't ever go to a psychiatrist; Christians should not ever, ever, ever, need mediation. Or the all-too-common "If you just had more faith," or "Just read this scripture and you will be well." Jesus doesn't want you depressed or worried. Jesus would never leave us in such a place of desperation. A Christian should never be thinking about suicide. Dear friend in Christ, if you are reading this book for yourself or planning on giving it to a friend in this dark, seemingly hopeless place, well then, you know this pain and have heard all these accusations. Makes me think of Job's friends standing around him trying to figure out why God is beating so heavy on Job. Well, I have some words for them and you. Don't be so quick to judge one if you have never walked a few inches in their shoes. Even as I am writing this introduction I am texting back and forth with a dear sister in Christ going through depression and anxiety, a wonderful woman in Christ yet struggling and feeling less of a Christian because she cannot climb out of this hole. I write this book for this very reason. I write it to open up the eyes of too many Christians who simply don't understand. Those who do not understand mental issues and the modern-day stresses and struggles that we face. The simple fact is this: If God doesn't want us to deal with or talk about mental illness in an open and frank way, then why is my counseling practice busting at the seams with two major areas—Christians who are dealing with depression and anxiety? The very fact that this is reaching epidemic proportions is a clear enough sign that we need help. Help, not judgment. We need a new fresh dialogue on what is going on and why so many of us are hurting. If Christians are thinking about suicide in increasing numbers, then someone must stand up and scream HELP and WHY! Someone must be willing to open up a too-long-hidden topic and cut away the cancer of lies and ignorance. Listen, I am a pastor and a Christian counselor. I love the Lord Jesus Christ with all my heart and soul, but I have and do struggle with depression and anxiety. I have struggled with it all of my life, but it only really came upon me full bore after I came to Christ. Now if I came to a saving knowledge of Christ and then I was dealt a stealth attack of desperation to the point that I was planning my own death, well, that means one of two things: God is not real and a lie, or God is real and very well alive but using my anxiety and depression as tools. Yes, tools in the Master's hands, tools of hope and new beginnings. So please, dear suffering friend, do not listen to the lies from the enemy and even the lies from good friends who just don't get it, people who mean well but can never understand the pain and anguish that comes with this veiled blessing. With all of my heart I plead with you to take my challenge and go through this book and yearly devotional sold separately. Take the time to listen to something I feel you have never heard before in regard to this taboo topic. Please listen and do not let my "coming out" on this issue be wasted or fall on deaf ears. I promise you a never seen before honesty and freshness, an approach that very few have ever taken in this area. I will share with brutal honesty my own story with all of its ugliness and darkest gloom. I will share my struggle with pride and shame and all that goes along with it, the days of wanting to give up, the days of being bedridden and unable to even function as a human. The days when sin seemed appealing and getting back at God and all my friends would somehow show them how real this is. The tears that flowed until there were none left to shed, the days of planning my own suicide as I felt that it was my only escape from this torment and pain—when just getting up in the morning would send chills of fear down my spine and sleep was my only desire. Then the fear that set in when even sleep would not offer me the escape I so desired and longed for. Or of the days when I even pondered if God was even real and my whole life in Christ was a sham. The days I would either be curled up in the fetal position in my bed or when I would pace the floors crying out to God, begging Him for deliverance. The days of asking Him, "Lord, where are You, why must I suffer so?" The days of reading my Bible, going to sleep with scripture playing, and yet no comfort. I tell you it is a pain like no other, a pain that was so tormenting that cancer or any other illness looked like a better way to go. In fact, I would often beg the Lord to give me some illness so at least I had a reason or excuse to feel so helpless. See the problem with mental illness is it is just that, something inside that no one sees. How many times people would say "You look fine to me." Oh, if they only knew, and that's just it, they never would know because it is truly a hidden torture of sorts. Also through this book I will take you through my highs and lows, my struggles with taking medication, debating about seeing a doctor or psychiatrist, days when I had to beg the Lord, "Please get me through this, I cannot do it alone." We will talk about the depression in its various forms, and anxiety in its own demonstrative variations. Panic attacks and the hot flashes, cold sweats, the numbness of limbs, the shortness of breath, then the heart pains and palpitations. Oh, this monster or blessing comes in so many forms, from mild to wild and everything in between. Then we will discuss the annoying roller coaster of feeling good then crashing. The thoughts that would constantly haunt me, thoughts like *Will this ever go away, will I ever be normal again?* Of the anger and sadness of watching a person doing a simple act like watering flowers and wondering, *Will I ever be able to enjoy those simple things?* Yes, depression makes you long for the simplest joys to be had again. Oh, to walk along the beach and smell the fresh fragrance of April hope. Again friends and fellow sufferers, no one can ever know this pain lest they endure it themselves. There is not an off or on switch as many would suggest to me, "Oh, just be happy." They would say, "You have so much" or "Just relax, God is in control." I tell you there were times when those words would eat at me with unbridled vengeance. I would often think or say, "Don't you think I would turn off this pain if I could?"

Yes, this monster of blessing is so dynamic in its execution and function, so varied and personal. I truly would not wish it on my worst enemy. So again, please hold on, dear friend, hold on till the end, the end of pain and the beginning of hope. Yes, there will be slipups and setbacks. Yes, friends and family will not be of much help sometimes. Yes, when medication is needed, there will be mockers from our Christian circles. I promise you the truth. I promise you the real deal and real life down and dirty application. Friend, I do not write this book for fame or fortune as most likely it will only bring me shame as my story goes public, but I will fall on God's Word where He says He will lift up the humble. There is always risk in sharing a deep, personal struggle with a sometimes impersonal and uncaring world. Like the risk I took when I wrote my first book, *Spiritual Living in a Sexual World*, and exposed my secret sin of sexual addiction to pornography. Yet of risk there really is none in Christ as Christ is the only one that I need to deal with. It is with Christ that all things pertaining to this life really have any meaning. Also I want to share with you what I will not be doing. See, my first thought was to give you all the stats on depression and then go deep into the theological debate and scriptural take on emotional issues. Yes, I will touch on them to some degree; but in the end what we all want, what you want, are answers, real answers of hope and power and promise of a better tomorrow. Well, that is one thing I do promise you, and not because my words have any meaning, but because God says it is so. God will never leave us, and God will never forsake us. Dear friend and child of God, my hope is that you will hold on one moment longer. Hold on just another day more. Listen to my words and the words of many of my patients and their stories that I will share. Listen to the end game and how it all turns out. Listen for God's still, small voice telling us to reach just a little bit further for He is there. Listen to God's voice telling you the truth about you, that He still loves you and knows every detail of your journey of faith. He is there. He is with you though He might seem so distant at times. May your "trial of faith" be pleasing to Him, knowing that nothing that falls upon us is wasted and is all under the control of the lover of our souls. He knows. He has a purpose and an outcome He wishes to achieve in you. As you might have noticed even through this brief introduction, the wording (i.e., "monster of blessings," "tool in the Master's hand"), I say these things because when you see what I want you to start seeing, that your own struggle is not a curse or punishment but a term of endearment. A gift, a tool and blessing so wonderful that it is only used on those the Lord has the most wonderful plans for. Our struggle as you will find is actually a door to a place and walk with Christ like no other. A place of intimate purpose and a closeness to God like no other. So many of us cry to hear from God and see Him in the now. Well, I stand here today proclaiming that through this emotional pain and struggle I have heard the voice of the Lord and met with Him in a very tangible way. He is real, He is alive, and He is working out our salvation in the daily affairs of men and women. He is there, and He knows and does not waste one moment of our pain. Are you ready? Are you fixed upon this painful yet glorious journey deep into the

Master's bosom? Please join me each day as we work through this blessed hope of emotional body building.

In Christ, fellow sufferer and child of God, Galatians 3:26

—S. R. Kraniak

Why Depression?
Yes, It Happens to Them Too!

Cursed be the day I was born! May the day my mother
bore me not be blessed!

—Jeremiah 20:14

Jeremiah is called the weeping prophet. Why? Well, for one, he
wept! It is strange that we as people of faith find it odd that
tears are part of that faith. It would be hard to find a place in
God's Word where tears, pain, and depression are not found. In
my years as a believer in Christ, I never thought, or even considered, what lie ahead for those that the Lord would use. I often
wonder if the apostles knew what would befall them as followers
of Christ. Would they be so quick to lie under His cross?

Depression

As I looked up the word *depression* in the *Webster's Dictionary*,
I was amazed to see the plethora of bombastic definitions. For
example, the definition ranged from being depressed; a hollow or
low place on a surface; low spirits; gloominess; sadness; a decrease
in force; a decrease in functional activity; area of relatively low
barometric pressure; low; an emotional condition characterized
by feelings of hopelessness, inadequacy.

From this description we can logically see that not all uses of the word *depression* is of the emotional type. Yet one thing is clear, *low* is at the center of the word. Whether it is a low in the economy or a dimple depression in the horizon, low is low. It is the opposite of high.

It is amazing the magnetic pull we have toward height. To be above is one of the first things we desire as children; to be on our father's shoulders, to be on top of the monkey bars at the playground. When the parade is coming down the street, we stretch our necks to see. That is what we really desire—to see! Yet what if seeing is not what we need. We know as parents our first reaction to a horrific scene on the television or to an automobile accident is to hide our children's eyes from it. Why? Why do we hide, or if I may bring low, our children's ability to see pain or horror? Is it not to keep them from that which they are not quite able to bear at such a young age? Maybe in not seeing one thing we are actually making them see another.

When I was first dealt the debilitating blow of depression, my first thought was to see higher. To see what the Lord was keeping from me. All of the joy and fun of the day was no longer in my grasp. It was as if my Heavenly Father was keeping my eyes from seeing what I so desperately desired to see: life, joy, the sun again. Why would a loving father keep me from seeing what I so desired to see? Again, maybe He wanted me to see from a new vantage point. Maybe He wanted me to see what could only be seen through forced perspective. Why, Lord? Why bring me low when high is where I long to live. Where high is, where the clouds dwell, and that is where I desire to live again. Well, I don't know if I ever lived in the clouds in the first place, but I certainly knew I desired to be there when depression took its hold.

Friend and fellow soldier of the wounded heart, I have been in the depths of depression, clinical depression, where the desire to live or even arise from my bed was hard to achieve. Yet through those times, which I considered the worst of times, I also consider them now the times that I could not have lived without. Depression is an odd thing. For all of its negatives, hidden beneath them are so many positives. Like I said earlier, a forced perspective is one, being able to see things that can only be seen in those dark low places. Feeling every breath that we so often take for granted. Thinking of God, heaven, and the meaning of life come oh so desired to be known. Watching others laugh and do simple things suddenly brings you great appreciation of those little things. Oh, to just stroll down the block and read the morning paper on a summer day, things that I never considered wonderful, yet at that place in depression they were wonderful. Oh, if I could only do them again. Oh, Lord, just to have a simple day of living.

So of depression, can it be evil if it brings good? Can the Lord not be a part of it if with it brings the deepest thoughts about Him you have ever felt (whether they be hateful or loving thoughts toward Him)? Jeremiah, Elijah, David, and so many others went through those days alone, those days of hating life itself, through those days of lying with their head toward the dry desert sands and watching an ant carrying its daily burden of crumbs. Can that not be used by God to do just as wonderful things in us as does the sunniest days? If we hate depression, we also hate what God does. We hate what tools He uses. If a mechanic repairs your automobile and his choice tool is a large hammer, shall we hate that hammer even though it is the tool that gets the job done?

In chapter 2 we will look deeper into this tool called depression, a tool truly in the Master's hand. If we hate it, we hate the one who also swings it. The hammer blows a crack at our soul, yet what if the repair needs that violent action? To be brought low, for whatever reason He chooses to bring it into your life, if He be the one who brings it, can we dare refuse it? My friend, no one swings that hammer for too long. If so, the metal beneath its blow would break and fatigue. A sinful man can over hammer, but the

Lord cannot. Do we trust Him that much to believe He knows the metal of soul and flesh that one who would swing too much would destroy? Dare to believe Him that much. Dare to believe He knows the last blow needed and not one more.

A Tool in the Master's Hand

*But now, O LORD, Thou art our Father; we are the clay, and
Thou our Potter; and we all are the work of Thy hand.*

—Isaiah 64:8

Dear friend, as we talk about depression today, we need to first
talk about tools. Please bear with me as I share my story about
tools. It might seem like I am dragging this point out too long,
but if you can read on and listen, you will understand why I spent
the time in setting up this object lesson.

Before I was a pastor and counselor, I was a mechanic. I come
from a long line of mechanics. My dad was one, my uncle, even
my father-in-law. I grew up as a little boy going to work at my
dad's auto repair shop. On special Saturdays my dad would take
me to work with him, and to me it was the most exciting place to
be. I think at age six or seven, I started going with him. At first
he would seat me in the back of the shop outside with my toy
trucks. When I was older, he would let me sit in the junk cars,
and I would pretend that I was driving them. At about thirteen
or so, I began to work the lifts up and down. Even getting to
sit in a car on a lift was a fun thing. Yet the one thing I would
always take from those days was the use of tools. Before I knew
it I was watching my dad fix cars, install new brakes and even
new engines. When I turned sixteen, my dad purchased for me
my first small set of professional grade tools, some of which I
still have to this day. Learning to use tools was something my

father taught me, and he would always say, "Use the right tool for the right job." If he would catch me pounding a screw in with a hammer or using a hammer for anything but that which it was made for, he would yell at me. "Don't be lazy, son!" He would say, "There is a special tool for special jobs." I was amazed at how many tools there were, and when I started to work as a young mechanic, my dad also got for me my first beat-up rolling toolbox. The first thing I did was fill it. When the tool salesman would come, I would quickly run up a large tab buying tools. I began to learn that there are specialty tools that are designed for only one purpose and one purpose only. They were so specialized that you rarely used them unless that one special need came up. They were the most expensive tools as they were custom made. In time, when those tools became too expensive for me, I learned the art of making my own tools. I would come upon a situation when no wrench or socket would work. I then would look carefully at the challenge ahead and then carefully take some scrap metal and an old tool and then heat it, bend it, cut it, and weld it so it became my own specialty tool for that special, and sometimes one-use, job, never to be used again.

Now maybe you are wondering why I am spending so much time talking about tools, or maybe you are even getting a bit impatient with my life story and the art of tool making, but it is all very important. Dear friend, the human mind and body are clearly well-designed machines. They take fuel in, and through that fuel, work and production come out. It is clear also that we were designed with a purpose far beyond having a good time and going to parties all the time. No, we were made to serve the Lord, to be vessels of honor who at the end of our days would have a long list of accomplishments for Him. If you live your life for anything less than Him, you are wasting your life and what you were created for. In Revelation 4:11 this is clearly defined, and I suggest you read it and understand it well. Now we being vessels and machines designed for His purpose, which *by the way are to bring Him Glory and tell others about His Salvation*, we are also prone to failure. That is another thing my dad used to tell me: "Any machine is prone to failure." The more complicated a machine, the greater chance of it breaking. That being the case, we are prone to breaking, and when we do in regard to using our minds and bodies for things other than God's glory, the Lord then must step in and do something to get us back on track. This is where the Lord opens up His celestial toolbox and looks for the proper tool for the particular area of trouble. In that toolbox the Lord has many tools. Some are common tools while some are specialty tools that He uses on a very particular problem to get a very particular result. The common tools are His hammer and chisel; these He uses on us daily for chipping away at the old, hard heart and creating in us a new heart. He also has in His toolbox the pry bar; this one is long and heavy as He needs it so large to help pry us away from the things that we will not let go of. Things like lust, hate, toys, possessions, and the desire to be important and famous. We have a hard time letting go of these things, so a pry bar is the only tool that will work. In some cases some damage is done because we held on so tightly to our possessions that some flesh and blood had to be broken to free us from them. Sometimes we feel the pry bar's pain through accidents, sickness, and even death of a loved one. Yet keep in mind, though, the tool may be different each time, but the goal is always the same, to get this human machine to do what it was made to do, bring people to Christ and glorify the Lord. For the most part these common tools work well, and we soon get the message and see that serving the Lord is only where we find true peace. We learn this because as soon as we let go of what we thought was so important, we suddenly feel a release and a newness of life. We feel this because we stop placing all of our energies into the wrong areas, and now we don't have to hold on so hard. In return we feel renewed and filled with energy and true peace and release. Like I said, these common tools work well for the most part and for most people, but for some of us the Lord has to open up that top drawer of His toolbox. In there, laid out on fine felt are His specialty tools. Ask any mechanic to show you his toolbox and he will show you that special drawer. Sometimes he even has that drawer locked as his most expensive tools are there and he is also less prone to lend out those tools. Now our Lord being the Master Craftsman, the Master Builder, the Master Healer, He has that drawer and laid out in it are some of these tools. To the left of the drawer is anxiety. It has prickly barbs and even He doesn't like to pick it up too often as it even hurts Him. He used that tool when Jesus was in the garden and began to sweat drops of blood in fear of what He would face. Then there is despair, worry, and all the way toward the right in a glass container, depression. Funny thing about this tool is it is not really that big or scary to look at; instead it is just a cold block of steel. All He has to do is place it on your life and all the warmth of our souls gets drawn out and into the block. This tool the Lord only uses when He wants a very special result. He would rather not use it, but it works so well that sometimes it's the only tool of choice. See, depression is like sleeping on a cold concrete basement floor. They say if you were to take a person and lay them naked on concrete or cement in a cold, dark basement, all their heat would be drawn out until death came. Now the Lord knows the risk of this particular tool, and He also knows the results. Of the results there is no question, of the risk there is great danger. The danger is leaving this cold block of steel on the heart for too long. If it be left there one minute too long, death to the soul can occur, but the good news is, God would never leave it on our soul past the point of no return. Again this tool is laid aside for special projects and for the most precious saints. People like Charles Spurgeon had this tool laid on him, as well as many other dear saints—Elijah, Job, David, and many others. Yet the results they brought forth could be accomplished no other way. In my life the Lord knew what tool was needed on me, which was depression, and what I had to do was simply trust the Master who held that tool. Honestly it was not the tool that scared me so much, but if I trusted the Lord enough to know what He was doing with it. In all honesty, there were times when

I did not trust Him and was sure He was leaving it on way too long. At other times I outright pushed it away in anger. I said, "Get that cold steel off me, you are killing me and you don't seem to care." Yet even with all my yelling and weeping, He would not, and I mistook His tardiness for neglect. Dear friend, this tool in the Master's hand is just that, a tool that must be used to bring about the most blessed results. It's the only tool in some circumstances that will do what needs to be done, and for that fact He uses it only on those in which He plans to do the most with. Again the trust issue is a big one, which makes me think about a time when I had a dangerous ear infection where possibly my eardrum might be damaged. So I went to a specialist who was well known for his skills and results. Now I was fine going to see him and felt good knowing that he was tops in his practice, but that was until he did something that I didn't quite like or trust him with. In fact I outright pushed him away. What he was doing was taking a small tube that had pressurized air being pumped through it. He moved it toward my ear to place it inside to push air into my ear canal. I didn't like that, and it felt more like I was going to be hurt than healed. After I pushed him away, he smiled and said, "What's wrong"? I told him, "What are you trying to do, kill me or blow out my eardrum?" He said, "Well, actually I am, but not how you are thinking." Little did I know that the ear, nose, and throat canals are all somewhat connected, and in extreme cases this actually helps. My problem was not his tool so much as trusting if he knew what he was doing with that tool. It is the same with the Lord, but oh, once we trust Him, watch what results it brings. Following are the wonderful results and growth wrought in my life through depression: *intimacy with the Lord*, such an intimacy can be had no other way; *maturity*, learning what's really of value and important in life; *power with God*, having the Lord's ear ever close to your request; *humility*, coming to that place where everything about me is torn out and thrown away until only Christ remains; *insight*, the ability to see what others don't see of God's will and work; *usefulness*, to be able and equipped for use in His most important matters; *vision*, seeing what I was never able to see before, to preach like I never preached before, to love like I never loved before. The list goes on and on, and because of these blessings, I can truly say, without my depression I would not be the man I am today. I would not be able to minister to others like I can today. I could not be made ready for what big plans He has in store for me today. All because of this blessed tool in the Master's hand called depression. Don't fight it or hate it, but welcome it as you would a vaccination. Sure it hurts going in, but it also makes you able to live in a disease-infected world without being affected by it. In closing on this matter, until you see depression as an honored gift from the Lord Himself, you will never reap the benefits of it. Yes, the blessed benefits of depression. To some a curse, but to those who see, a wonderful tool that makes us ready for His service in ways we never thought possible.

Gain Through Pain

And if children, then heirs; heirs of God, and joint-heirs with Christ; if so be that we suffer with Him, that we may be also glorified together.

—Romans 8:17

I don't know about you, but I hate to suffer. I don't even like to stub my toe, yet I know I will again and again. As long as I have toes and there are things on the floor and ground, toes will be stubbed. Now in our chapter for today, we are going to talk about this: *gain through pain*, good coming from suffering. Now I know what many of you are thinking—not another flowery-filled poetic object lesson with cryptic imagery. I don't blame you. There are so many books and quotes written about the virtue and blessings of hard, tough things. Why add another? It seems like every time we fall or suffer, there is someone there with a corny statement such as "Well, you have fallen, but that just means God is going to pick you up" or "The harder we fight, the higher we achieve." I could go on and on because sometimes people don't know when to stop with the life quotes. I remember a person from church becoming furious after going through a great loss and another person coming up to them and saying, "Well, it is not about 'why you,' but 'why not you'"? Now the person doing the so-called comforting thought they were helping, but sometimes it is the wrong time to say the right thing. Today I will try to not make that same mistake, which is not easy to do. Talking about pain and suffering in our lives is not something most people want to hear about. Today if you are suffering with depression and anxiety, you don't want to hear about how helpful it is but when it is going to be gone. Why is it even here and why must you suffer with it? Dear fellow sufferers, I'm right there with you, and I know about suffering, especially emotional suffering. When I was dealt my hand of anxiety and depression, the last thing I wanted to do was praise the Lord and shout Glory unto His name. Instead I was angry, bitter, sad, and asking God why me? Why now? Emotional trauma is like that. It is the worst kind of pain. It is silent pain and pain that we cannot accept much sympathy for. People just don't get it or understand it unless they have gone through it. What we must do is resign ourselves to the fact that for now our pain is here, no one will understand it, but that somehow we will and must make it through. For me this was very important and still is. Thoughts of giving up must be forgotten, and you must accept the current situation. If we love God and trust Him, then we must be willing to follow Him even if He leads us to the town landfill for breakfast. In John 18:11 we get some good advice from Jesus Himself about accepting something painful for the time being even if it is not pretty: "*The cup which my Father hath given Me, shall I not drink it?*" Here Jesus is explaining to His disciples, who are trying to defend Him from the soldiers, that He needs no defending, that if God the Father deems it best for Jesus to go to the cross and be taken prisoner, then should He refuse it? I know, easy for Jesus to say, but with Christ dwelling in us, we need to be able to say the same thing. In my struggles it was not until I came to that place of acceptance that the Lord really took over. For so long I was the other way—demanding deliverance and saying I am not going to play nice, Lord, until you take this away. I was in effect telling the Lord that I was calling the shots and that my rules must be followed if anything is going to change. Well, God doesn't play by my rules as I soon found out, and if anything was going to change, it was going to have to start with me. *Submission* was the watchword that the Lord laid in my lap. Either I submit to the plans the Lord has for me or it will continue as is.

Now though I told you I wouldn't use cliché imagery, well, forgive me because I have to use at least one, and this is one that I know to be true. In my years as a mechanic—first, automotive; then diesel; then heavy earth-moving equipment—the one thing I learned that was a mandatory skill was welding. I wasn't a very good welder at first, but in time I was. I knew I had to be better because when I did weld something and it fell apart, it only made more work for me in redoing old repairs. One of my mistakes in welding was penetration and heat control. In order to weld properly, you must stick that welding rod deep in the V, which is where the weld is going, and the next was having the proper heat setting on your welder to bring it all together. Now if you don't know what welding is, it's taking two sections of metal and making them one. It is a hot, messy, loud procedure if it is to be done right. Preparing the sections to be welded together is also important. If you do not clean out the welding area, dirt will cause voids, and the weld will not hold. One other thing about welding is this. It is said that a good weld is stronger than the metal itself, meaning that the repaired section is the best and strongest section. So what does this all have to do with depression and emotional trauma? What does this all have to do with looking at depression as something good and not evil? Well, it actually fits perfect because as welding is a necessary evil to fix something that's broken, so is depression necessary to repair what's broken in us, which in most cases is our relationship with God. The Lord is one section of metal, and our *wills* and desires are another. If we don't bond properly, it will not hold, and it will not be strong enough to do the work the Lord has planned for us. So what the Lord must do is weld us together with Him so to speak so that our union is stronger than anything else in our lives. As in welding preparation is critical, so is preparation in spiritual union with the Lord. First, the painted, rusted parts must be ground away with a powerful grinder. Sparks fly, metal chips are all over, and the noise is bone chilling. In our lives, before the Lord can bond through depression, He must clean us out. He must grind away all the impurities that separate us from Him. In the case of people, it is our sin that is the problem. Now one would think that cleaning that sin out is enough, but it leaves some bare, exposed nerve endings that if not covered quickly with the Holy Spirit, new sins can begin to grow. This is where the Holy Spirit welding begins. The Lord heats up things until its cherry red. Then He lays in His welding rod, which fills in the gaps between man and Lord. It too is a loud, painful process, and the metal itself seems to want to cry out as it is forced to join with another, but when the process is done, and if it is done well, we have two that become one. Two *wills* that are now one will, and that union is so bonded together that it becomes the strongest part of us. In Psalm 30:5 we see a picture of Holy Spirit welding, the pain of the process but also the result of the process. "*For His anger endureth but a moment; in His favor is life: weeping may endure for a night, but joy cometh in the morning*" (Psalm 30:5).

Some may question if this is the best way to join us forever with the Lord's will, and why can't the Lord use another. I will answer that question simply by saying, because this way makes the strongest bond. As in welding, I have gotten lazy at times, and instead of going through the labor of welding a broken part, I tried using epoxies, glues, and other lesser means, only to have it fall apart in a short time. In some cases, almost hurting or possibly killing people who were depending on that part to hold. Why do we repel so much the methods of welding? It is simply because welding and the procedure is a lot like suffering. Both sections of metal must suffer as they let go of their independence and become one with the other. We simply don't like to let go of who we are, our comfort zone, our level of spirituality that we feel comfortable with. We really don't want a deeper relationship with the Lord. We say we do but refuse to take the steps needed to make it real. Those steps again often include depression /welding. Suffering is a part of this, and so we shy away from it.

Yet if any man suffer as a Christian, let him not be ashamed; but let him glorify God on this behalf. (1 Peter 4:16)

For what glory is it, if, when ye be buffeted for your faults, ye shall take it patiently? but if, when ye do well, and suffer for it, ye take it patiently, this is acceptable with God. (1 Peter 2:20)

If we suffer, we shall also reign with Him: if we deny Him, He also will deny us. (2 Timothy 2:12)

So many scriptures speak of this suffering process and yet still we want nothing to do with it. We want the results without the effort, we want the strength of metal that comes from welding, but we don't want to be welded. Dear friend, until we see depression for what it is, we will only see it as an evil force set to destroy all that we are and know. Sure some depressions are more intense; some are of the chemical, clinical type; but at the end of the day, it is still depression, and if we be a child of God by faith in Jesus Christ, then it too has purpose. So the next question must be, how do we let God weld us together with Him? How do we live through this process if it be so painful? Well, first thing is to not fight it as much as listen while you are in it. Listen for the Lord's still, small voice and what He might be trying to tell you. While you are doing this, begin the necessary steps of finding out what type of depression you have and how severe it is. That would mean going to a counselor, therapist, psychologist, or even your family doctor at first. In a perfect world I would seek out Christians in those fields, but that is not always possible. Listen to what they have to say, and though this may seem odd, I would not mention to them much about the spiritual dynamic of your life as they are trained sometimes to classify you in a certain way and see your faith in God or your spirituality as part of your problem. This is sad to say, but it is true. For the most part finding a Christian counselor is not the hard part, it is finding a Christian psychiatrist or psychologist that is hard. Just be careful in the process and listen to what they tell you but always put a God filter on it all, making sure their advice is not contrary to the Word of God.

As you begin to digest all the information you are getting from these mental health care providers, also keep a tab on the information that the Lord is giving you. Taking notes and or keeping a journal is not a bad idea. Reading a devotional and the Bible as much as possible is also the key to hearing what the Lord is trying to tell you. As for church, *go!* So many people who are going through depression seem to have the same foolish plan and reasoning. They will decide to stop going to church until they work things out in their minds. Then when all is back to normal, they will get back to church like they used to. This, my friend, is part of Satan's trick, to unplug you from your life source. Sadly this is the worst thing you can do, which can only be likened to bleeding through a major wound and saying; "As soon as I get better, I will visit the hospital ER." How foolish that would be, and how foolish are we if we stop going to church at the very time we need to hear from the Lord the most. My advice is maybe even to use this time to find the right church that the Lord has planned for you, a good Bible-believing, nondenominational Christian church. Not so much one with a lot of *circus appeal* but one that is more concerned about the Word of God and teaching it with all its hardness at times. You need a tough-love church where the people and pastor care more about pleasing God than keeping their church-building program funded, a church where saying what must be said is more important than saying what people want to hear.

As the process of your spiritual welding continues, also make sure you have a life partner that knows what you are going through, either a spouse or a trusted Christian friend who knows to keep an eye on you. Give them updates as to your progress and your ups and downs. Make sure you don't begin to slip too far into depression because you can reach a point where the benefits of it start to fade and the negatives of it begin to increase.

If your depression goes into clinical mode—meaning bedridden, lack of desire to live or do anything—then you might want to consider medication through your doctor. The medication is not to heal you as much as it is to keep you from falling too far, and though it can heal you to some degree, only the Lord will give you peace. Trust in Him alone and never the medication. Look at the medication as only a tool that God is using and never the salvation. All in all remember what the Bible says over and over again about our present suffering—whether it is emotional, financial, or physical—gain always comes from pain. Maybe not what you want to hear, but it's a fact of life no matter where you go. Just look at a body builder, they only look the way they do because they agonized under the heavy weights and hours of exercise. They didn't get that way from looking at the exercise equipment but by using it and using it hard and long. I wish there was another answer to your present pain, but I have found all that I have said today to be true. It is not just believing in Jesus Christ or going to church or reading your Bible, but it is also being willing to suffer as He calls you to suffer. It will be good because only good can come from God.

For unto you it is given in the behalf of Christ, not only to believe on Him, but also to suffer for His sake. (Philippians 1:29)

Anxiety That Kills vs. Anxiety That Saves

*The fear of man bringeth a snare: but whoso
putteth his trust in the LORD shall be safe.*

—Proverbs 29:25

Anxiety is something that appears to be growing faster than the national debt. In my years of counseling, I have never seen anything like what I am seeing today. It's not just in my practice but in all the churches that I am friendly with, and counseling associates. There are many things that are quite odd about this plague as I like to put it. For one thing it is how fast it is spreading and the nature of the anxiety itself. My associate that I use for all the medication needs of my patients is a state-certified psychiatrist, and we often share our perplexity over this plague upon the land. From teens to children, male and female, the only ones who seem to be somewhat immune to it is our elderly, which battle more with depression. Of the nature of the anxiety is what I find so fascinating because it's a type of anxiety that is affecting those who have never had anxiety before. People who were once rock solid, be it Christian or non-Christian, are now feeling this twinge of what I like to call "something is coming anxiety," or SICA. It is not a fear of losing a job or getting cancer or what have you, but a fearful and unsettling feeling that impending doom is upon us. I have heard people say things like "Something is just not right, it is as if the earth or the cosmos changed its rotation." Where once they had peace and looked forward to vacations, new jobs, fun-in-the-sun future, and retirement, now they have a sense of apprehension about things. I think Christians seem to have a better understanding as they have the Holy Spirit, which is somehow poking them as if to warn them, yet of what they do not know. People are coming in and simply saying, "I am just not myself, things are not business as usual anymore."

We are going to spend some time on this SICA phenomenon, and from there we will deal with the various other forms of anxiety—what they are, what they mean, and what they can and cannot do to you. We will talk about panic attacks and what they are all about. Also we will talk about treatments—what works and doesn't work. We will talk about the anxiety that cripples us and the anxiety that can actually help us. We will also discuss the symptoms of anxiety as they are often confused with other issues like depression. If they are confused, then mistreatment can happen, leading to more trouble than you started with. We will also go over diet and the simple steps you can take to speed up your recovery. Anxiety is a very complex beast, and to beat it or at the least live with it takes some doing. Sometimes even mental health care providers miss the real nature of our anxieties, and if they be not Christian, they will certainly have a more difficult time understanding the spiritual aspect of it. So I ask you to follow along with me as we go through the quantum dynamics of anxiety—a monster from Satan or a messaging system from the Lord?

SICA

True, it is not a scientific or even psychological term, but it is what I have been seeing a lot of lately. This feeling that things are not as they were and will not ever be again is something that in the spiritual realm seems to be emanating. Not to go into eschatology, which is a study of future biblical things, we cannot discount the fact that the world is changing. Things are not as they once were. Nations are rising against nations and troubles are on every shore. God's anger has been kindled, and His peace and blessing upon our land seems to be departing. When this happens either in the future or in the past, the results are the same: God is removed and fear comes in.

"*Thus saith the Lord GOD; I will also destroy the idols, and I will cause their images to cease out of Noph; and there shall be no more a prince of the land of Egypt: and I will put a fear in the land of Egypt*" (Ezekiel 30:13). It is not so much that the Lord is making people afraid but that His anger and the lack of desire for Him causes us to trust in other things. These other things cannot bring peace, and so the result is anxiety. In Lamentations 3:46–50, we see how the Lord's absence allows our enemies' presence. Result again is fear but on a national level.

All our enemies have opened their mouths against us.

Fear and a snare is come upon us, desolation and destruction.

Mine eye runneth down with rivers of water for the destruction of the daughter of My people.

Mine eye trickleth down, and ceaseth not, without any intermission,

Till the LORD *look down, and behold from heaven.*
(Lamentations 3:46–50)

All over the Bible we see this national fear of an angry God. In Jeremiah 49:23–24 we see in greater detail this fog like rolling in of fear.

Concerning Damascus. Hamath is confounded, and Arpad: for they have heard evil tidings: they are fainthearted; there is sorrow on the sea; it cannot be quiet.

Damascus is waxed feeble, and turneth herself to flee, and fear hath seized on her: anguish and sorrows have taken her, as a woman in travail. (Jeremiah 49:23–24)

We can go on and on, but the fact remains, in the last days of the church there will be a fear that rolls over the land, and it might even fall upon our own hearts if we are not drenched in His Word and rock solid upon His firm foundation. Dear friend, let not your heart be troubled. Yes, there shall be tribulation in the land and of that it is certain, but Jesus also told us: "Be of good cheer, I have overcome the world." So of this national fear, this SICA (something is coming anxiety), we need to let that go and know that that fear is not for us if we be children of God through faith in Jesus Christ. Wars will come, economies will tumble, and sin will run rampant in the land, but these things must be. Just as Jesus went to the cross so we could be set free from sin, so must national tribulations come so that we can be delivered from.

Remember we are His bride, and if His bride, then without a doubt a people who will be protected and loved even in the worst of times. The Lord will not forsake His own no matter what, so let that national, spiritual fear depart from us and instead let it, if anything, remind us that the Word of the Lord is true, and if true, then trouble might come, but peace will come with that trouble for those who love Him, for those who look forward to his coming.

Anxiety in Many Forms

One of the problems with anxiety is trying to figure out if you actually have it and what are the symptoms of it. One of the most common scenarios is this, which I have seen over and over again: you begin to feel not right, something is wrong, so you start to try to figure out what you might have. You never think it is an anxiety issue even when many are telling you it is. Denial is a big part of anxiety, and until we include it in the possibilities list, we will forever miss it while spending a lot of money on medical tests simply because you don't want it to be anxiety. Like I said, you will see all types of specialists, take all kinds of tests, even go to the ER a few times swearing you have heart issues. Many doctors will play the game and put you through a battery of tests. Maybe it is your sugar, or a problem with your endocrine system, heart problems, brain tumor, circulation problems, allergies, thyroid—you name it you will chase after it. I know because I did the same thing. I would actually pray that some test would come back positive so I could tell everyone: "See I told you I was sick." But test after test will come back negative, and with each one your anger and your despondency will grow. Pride has a lot to do with diagnosing anxiety simply because of the stigma that comes with it. For some reason, we believe, and maybe rightly so, that people will lose some respect for us if our ailment all along was anxiety and not high blood pressure. Everything and anything in the realm of physical diseases are okay, but anything to do with our emotions seems to be taboo. It is so sad, and it is why people only get worse because they wait until the anxiety seeds have been planted and taken root. At that stage it becomes harder to uproot it. Thinking patterns have been developed, and responses have already been programmed. Please, dear friend, remember this—anxiety is very common today in both men and woman. It is no big deal, so accept it quickly and get healed just as fast. Wait too long and you might never be fully freed from its hold. Its tentacles are like that of alien monsters that slither around our bodies and find footholds in every crevasse. Once there, you need hundreds of tiny crowbars to remove them. Okay, so we know to consider anxiety as a possibility of why you are feeling the way you are, but what are the symptoms so we can know for sure?

Following are classic symptoms, some are textbook, most are from dealing with people with the condition, and some have been my own personal experiences. Just keep in mind that some symptoms are similar to medical issues, so do not discount a medical condition but also do not discount an emotional one.

Symptoms

Where do I begin to tell this story, there is just so much to tell as each person has a hybrid of sorts of anxiety-based symptoms. First, let us start with the simple beginning stages and then work up to full-blown anxiety and then into panic attacks.

1. A sense of unease, which is mostly felt near your heart area though it has nothing to do with your heart. It is like the feeling you get when you were a kid and you swam in a pool too long. Take a deep breath and you feel this cool heaviness. It is a feeling of not being able to quite catch your breath fully. It is always feeling like your breaths have become shortened and your breathing cycle is not right. The more you think about it, the more you try to regulate your breathing, which only leads to more anxiety as now you are trying to regulate your breathing consciously when it should be done subconsciously.

2. A tingling feeling on the palms of your hands and on the bottoms of your feet. Remember not all of these symptoms will always be the same or all at once. Different people feel and experience it in different ways sometimes. It could be numbness in your arms, sometimes actually a locking up feeling, cold or hot sweats that can be mild to a drenching sweat bath, almost like someone turned on your sweat pump. Confusion is also another one as our mind tries so hard to focus on its daily movements but is distracted by this new feeling it has never had before. Suddenly little tasks become big tasks. Tripping and being clumsy are now a part of you. Retaining your focus on a task also becomes an issue simply because your brain can only do so many things at one time. The result of this inward battle is physical exhaustion where you become so tired that falling asleep at work or while reading become normal. You go from great heights of agitation to complete falls into lethargic episodes. What's amazing is

DEPRESSION, ANXIETY, AND THE CHILD OF GOD

that most people around you won't notice much of this as it is all a battle on the inside. We may feel like the world is watching our inward mind with a camera, but they are not, nor can they.

3. Anger and agitation become a new part of your personality. You begin to have a very short temper and fuse. Outbursts of rage may happen in some people, but in others the complete opposite, like becoming reclusive and falling into agoraphobia (wanting to stay inside). Fear of large crowds and noisy, busy places begin to irritate you. Little noises like tapping and loud sharp noises also annoy you. Hypersensitivity to sound is very normal. Lashing out at people for reasons you cannot understand and then later regretting, having meltdowns about silly things that normally wouldn't bother you.

4. Eating changes, like loss of appetite that is so great that large amounts of weight are lost in a short time, or the opposite, increased appetite, which will lead to weight gain. In either case, stomach issues will be a problem, either with more frequent and looser bowel movements to heartburn and indigestion. Our stomach simply tries to counter all the stress by pumping all the excess chemicals being produced through our anxiety into our stomach. Our acid production becomes so high that ulcers can be formed. This is also another confusing symptom as many times people think their problem is a gastrointestinal one and seek the care of a gastroenterologist. This might treat those issues but only pushes the anxiety into another area of the body. In my life, my anxiety started years ago with stomach issues, always having cramps even as a child, which I thought was IBS. It became so bad that I couldn't go too far from a bathroom at any given time, and so I focused on fixing my cramping and diarrhea. In time I did correct that, which only moved my anxiety into my upper stomach, which produced horrible heartburn, which turned into an ulcer. Once the ulcer and heartburn were fixed, the

anxiety needed another new place to be realized, and having none, it materialized itself into the typical anxiety symptoms that I shared earlier. For years it was like chasing a chicken without a head. Simply pushing anxiety around from one place to another in my body but never really dealing with the core of the problem, which was anxiety itself.

5. Perpetual daily anxiety. I liken this to simply having or being in a state of mild anxiety all day, every day, with bouts of severe anxiety with or without panic attacks. This can be the most troublesome as it never seems to go away completely, and because of that fact, it is more prone to lead to depression. This type of anxiety is not due to an event or situation you are facing but simply anxiety for no known reason at all. It is anxiety because you have anxiety. You get up in the morning and check yourself to see how you are feeling; then by doing that self-test, you remind yourself that you are not okay and you kick in the anxiety again. For the most part you wake up okay, but thinking about it brings it on again. It is a heavy feeling like you feel you might cry at any moment. Again this type of anxiety leaves you exhausted at the end of the day and desiring sleep. It really does wear you down, which is why it's the door to depression. "If I am like this all the time, life isn't worth living," you conclude, and you fall into depression.

6. Situational anxiety. This is common and in most cases normal. It is becoming apprehensive when facing a trying day, a test, a challenge, or traveling to a place you have never been to before, getting married, buying a home, investing your money. Most people have anxiety from these, but for those who have some type of anxiety disorder, it becomes more acute and limiting. It is taking that "normal situational anxiety" and multiplying it by ten. Starting a new job now becomes impossible because the anxiety is not controllable and so your emotions become unmanageable. Having an amazing opportunity to give an important speech is now out of the question. This is when we know we have a problem that must be dealt with.

Dear friends, when anxiety stops you from being and doing what you were meant to do, this is when anxiety becomes a real issue and a tool in Satan's hand, a tool to take you away from all that God has called you to. It is a tool he uses to convince you that the Word of God is a lie, as in "You can do all things through Christ which strengthens you" (Philippians 4:13). All of a sudden we cannot believe that scripture and all of a sudden Satan wins. This is the dirty little secret about anxiety. It is the true motive behind the scenes. It has the ability, if we let it, to get us to question the Lord's Word. If we question one part, then we question it all. It is a slippery slope that I have lived on for many years. It has kept me back from the greater things of God until I chose to say "No, I will not listen to these lies!" God's Word is true, so my anxiety cannot stop me from doing what I am called to do. I tell you, anxiety comes and it goes, but what we allow it to do to us is up to us. Yet in the worst stages of anxiety, and I am talking paralyzing anxiety, I have performed weddings, done funerals, led people to Christ, counseled people dealing with depression and anxiety, raised a family, went on trips, ran a church, spoke at town council meetings, chaired boards, and oversaw church business meetings. No one ever knew what I was going through, yet in Christ I was able to be carried through these hard times. Now you might ask, "Well, do I have to look forward to a life trapped in anxiety?" No, you do not as I have spent most of my life in remission, but when needed, the Lord allows it to rear its wonderful, ugly head. Yeah, I said, wonderful ugly head. We have to look at anything that comes into our lives as good if we are really to trust the Lord Jesus Christ and have the victory.

Depression or Anxiety

I tell you, this is a great dilemma in the psychological world, separating anxiety from depression and depression from anxiety. Are they the same? Are they somehow codependent on each other?

These are questions that some will deny, but to those who are honest we will declare we really don't know. In my life of glorious suffering, I have had acute cases of both of them. Sometimes at the same time, and sometimes completely separate and distinct from each other.

In my particular situation and many others, the anxiety came first and led to depression. In fact my problem has always been anxiety feeding off obsessive-compulsive disorder. When left unchecked and unidentified, one spilled over into the other. The result was clinical depression of the worst kind. It is ugly, dark, and very hard to get out of alone. The key for me was to go after the anxiety with guns blazing, and in time the depression would go away on its own. Now that doesn't mean that depression is not a stand-alone condition and one we will go into further down the line. But it does mean that we must be very careful in treating the right cancer. Just as we wouldn't give someone cholesterol medication for high blood pressure, we shouldn't treat depression as we would anxiety or vice versa. In my second battle with emotional issues, it was my family doctor who made the bad call and kept moving me around on different depression medications, actually escalating my anxiety with each change. We must understand that depression medications, with the exception of one or two, do not help with anxiety, but in many cases they actually increase anxiety. In my case the more depression meds I was on, the worst my anxiety became, which led to more depression. The doctor focused on the depression as a more serious issue, so he gave me more depression medication. Talk about a mess of the worst kind. It wasn't until a good friend and associate who was also a psychiatrist found out that I was hurting and asked me what I was taking. It didn't take him too long to see that I never really had depression in the classic sense but only depression fueled by my anxiety. The medication was what was killing me in an emotional sense. Carefully I had to be taken off all that I was on, which was no easy task. I was so emotionally weak at that time that I almost didn't pull out of it. Some other meds were introduced to keep me stable until I was able to function properly again. Now putting all of my personal issues aside, my point is this: be very careful in treating or getting treatment for yourself. No matter if you take the holistic, medical, or spiritual route or all three. Just make sure you are treating the right issue. Yes, depression and anxiety have many similar traits and symptoms and can be extremely hard sometimes to pinpoint. Here is where a well-trained counselor is vital as they can spot the telltale signs and sift out the incorrect signs.

Treatments

Treating anxiety can be a daunting task. Many times it needs to be tackled from many different areas at once. For starters we need to find out what is the core cause of our anxiety. Is it real, imaginary, physical, spiritual, or psychological? Again, a good counselor might be needed to help you find your root cause, and a Christian counselor in my opinion can do it best. As to treatments I always like to go after the easy stuff first. Diet is a good place to start. Sugar, caffeine, sugar substitutes, and many other foods cannot only make things worse but actually create anxiety. In dealing with a young male teen who was struggling with anxiety, the first thing I asked him was if he was drinking any of those popular energy drinks. In fact he was, and even more he was addicted to them. I could write another book on the horrors of those drinks. Stay away from them!

As to sugar, it is a no-no in my book. Besides its quiet lifts, it also has crashing falls. I personally am on a no-sugar diet as it has a powerful effect on me. Caffeine, well, it can be a monster and a prince at the same time. Caffeine in many regard is a wonder drug, meaning that I wonder what it really does. Sure it can increase anxiety, but in some cases it can decrease anxiety as it improves your mood. In most cases it does not, but with some people it can help with anxiety and depression. In any case, check your level of caffeine intake and start off by removing it first. Over-the-counter medications can be another problem. Take cold and flu medications, for example, many of the decongestants on the market can set your anxiety soaring through the roof. Stay away from them. Painkillers like the ones being sold on the street today can also set your anxiety into orbit. As to herbal supplements I have nothing against them. Your best bet is a good nutritionist. As to vitamins, there are many that can help. Double-check your Bs, folic acid, and so on, but in most cases unless you have super-mild anxiety, I don't see much benefit here.

Anxiety for the most part is part of everyone's life but add the stresses of today's hectic world and a bit of OCD and you're a prime candidate for severe anxiety.

At the first acknowledgment that you have some level of anxiety disorder or even a simple season of your life where it is beginning to show, go to the Lord ASAP. I cannot emphasize enough the importance of prayer. The Lord our God is the Healer and our Guide, and we cannot beat any of these issues without Him. Confessing our sins and making sure we are where we are supposed to be in our spiritual walk should be high on our to-do list. See what the Lord might be trying to show you about yourself through your anxieties. What are they pointing to that we would not have seen without the anxiety? Reading scripture, daily devotional texts, and quiet time with the Lord is mandatory. One of the things this wonderful new world of technology has done is keep us far away from the Lord. Get out to the beach, mountains, or any wilderness. If you live in the city, then get alone on the rooftop of a high-rise and look at the stars and contemplate His wonders. Praise the Lord for all He is and what He is trying to show you.

Now before I move onto medications and if they are truly for the Christian, I would first like to speak about physical exercise. I know we all hate exercise and would rather not do it, but the fact that you hate it might mean that you need it. I'm personally not a big exercise person as I see how if taken to the extreme it can actually lead people into a self-love of sorts. Today we see more people at a gym on a Sunday morning than in church. Truly we love our bodies more than the Lord sometimes, and of that we must be very careful. With that said, that doesn't mean exercise doesn't play a role. In my first bout with depression and anxiety, exercise was helpful. I would come home from work and either get on my treadmill or ride my mountain bike in the wooded area where I lived. Back then cassette players were all that we had, so with some good praise music and a headset, I would pump away. In regard to exercise, weight training is not the preferred method but instead a good cardio workout. Getting your heart pumping until a good amount of sweat is pouring from your pores is best. There must be a releasing of chemicals and a transfer of brain signals. All that happens when our heart is really pounding is a great aid to our moods and tension-releasing healing faculties. It is said that in the Russian prison camps of years gone by, they did involuntary experimentation with the prisoners who suffered from depression and anxiety. The harder they physically labored, the better they were emotionally. Go figure, but exercise is a great way to burn off excess stress and nervousness. Again with that said, there is always an exception to the rule, and in some cases people become more anxious. Dear friend, all of this is a crapshoot of sorts as nothing works exactly the same for each person. If the Lord wants us to stay in that state of anxiety because we are in deep sin, then we could peddle a bike until we dropped dead with still no healing. One last thing, sex always is a topic today, and one might wonder where it fits in or does not fit in with emotional healing. Is an orgasm good or bad? Well, that depends on what we are talking about. If you are depressed, then most likely sex won't be on your mind, though I would suggest it. The chemical explosion that happens at both male and female orgasm is almost as mysterious as what is in mothers' milk. As to anxiety and orgasms, well, it is most likely to cause anxiety but again each case is different. If anything, it is at least an escape from the issue though momentarily, and it just might help. As the avid fishermen say, "There is no such thing as a bad day of fishing."

Now with all of those things in place that I just mentioned, that doesn't mean they will always deliver you alone. I know I stand on questionable ground when I say this, but medication can help. When I say questionable, I mean in the form of Christians questioning me on my pointing to medications. Now I will deal with the great debate of Christians and medications in another chapter, but I will tell you here and now no matter what anyone may say, if the Lord gave science the ability to find meds that lower our blood pressure, then could He not give meds that can help our anxiety issues? Dear friend, if you are suffering from major anxiety disorder where it has left you almost nonfunctioning, then it might be time to get help from the medical profession. Doctors are not demons and psychiatrists are not Satan, for the most part. If you have prayed over your issue and have had the elders of your church pray over you and anoint you with oil as per scripture, if you have taken every spiritual route that the Bible has given us and have done all those things and waited in faith for healing and it has not come, then maybe the Lord is telling us that our healing from Him will come through the medical community. Let us not be like the cults out there who let their loved ones die simply because they incorrectly interpret the scriptures and refuse a blood transfusion. This is foolishness and should act as a warning to us all. Listen, if we will quickly run to the doctor with an infected ear and have no problem with taking antibiotics to heal that ear, then we are hypocrites if we refuse antianxiety medication or antidepression medication.

In the realm of anxiety medication, there is a bit more of a warning about taking them to some degree. True, you can get addicted to them, and transfer your trust from the Lord into them. With many of the tranquilizer type meds, I strongly urge caution as they can place us in a state of intoxication. If you have to live in a fog due to medication, then that medication is not helping you heal but replacing God with another spirit. Yet in regard to today's breakthroughs, there are some new medications that are not tranquilizers but actually enable the body and mind to reduce the anxiety-causing chemical reactions to subside in our mind and body. They cause no drugging effect or fogginess. They don't make you sleepy for the most part and might just be the rung in the ladder that helps you climb out of the pit you are in and unto complete recovery. One day you can come off them and live medication free. Again, many Christians argue that faith alone is the answer, well, to them I reply, "Next time you need an appendix surgery as yours is ready to explode, just have faith in God to heal it." Yes, He does heal our inflamed appendix but through the hands of a skillful surgeon that He has raised and created. Please, people, let us not be pious fools who live by a double standard when it comes to medical treatments: one standard for physical ailments and another for emotional ailments that may just be because of physical conditions anyway. The brain is a complicated organ, as is the heart. They both work on many levels through a vast array of systems and signals. If our brain isn't firing properly and our chemicals are in disarray, then why can't it be treated with medication? If I could choose to live a life in emotional pain without medications or live a life of joy and peace again through God's hand by medication, who then is the fool and who is not walking by faith? What if the Lord is asking us to take meds and we don't due to our pride, who can we then blame for our pain?

Living daily in a state of anxiety is a horrible, horrible way to live, leaving life dark and horrific. Please do not judge a person who only wants to serve the Lord through any means the Lord deems proper for that person. We could also take the best medications that are out there, but if the Lord has us in a state of anxiety due to our sin life, we could take meds until the cows come home and still find no relief.

Panic Attacks / Anxiety Attacks

These two terms are used often as separate entities, but at the end of the day it is just semantics. Panic and anxiety, whether they are attacks or syndromes, are by nature very similar in their DNA.

An attack of any type is something that no one wants. They are sudden, crippling, and always leave us wounded. As to panic and anxiety attacks, they are a monster of their own. What's interesting about these types of attacks, no matter what you choose to call them, is that they don't always accompany anxiety disorder. Take a person who has just been through a horrific personal trauma. Say they were in a very bad car accident or molested, or raped. These events by nature can turn on the panic system in our bodies even if we have never suffered with them before. Always remember this: depression, anxiety, and panic attacks are not simply useless reactions. The Lord when He created us built into our magnificent bodies fail-safe and alarm systems. They have purpose, and we must only find out what they are. When a red light goes off on your car's dashboard, it doesn't mean that the dashboard has a problem but that your car does. The dashboard is doing what it was made to do—warn you. At its core, a panic attack during a life-threatening event is actually a good thing. If the roof of your home caves in during a hurricane and your children are in danger, the Lord ignites this super burst of energy and focus to do almost supernatural things. Your body is pumped and ready to fight an army. Its chemicals are pumping and your muscles are becoming stronger. In the racing world when one is losing a race, many engine builders install a system called nitrous oxide injection. They push a hidden red button and *whoosh*. They inject their engine with more horsepower, and they beat the other car. Our Lord has made our bodies in a similar way but now imagine having that same car while it's parked in your garage and someone pushes that injection button when the car isn't going anywhere. This is exactly what a panic attack is. It is our body being injected with chemicals for battle when there is no battle to fight. That is why most people after an attack only want to sleep. Their body thinks they just went ten rounds with a prize fighter when they were only standing in line at the checkout counter. So the problem is not what the body is doing but why it's releasing it at the wrong time. That is why medication can be so helpful in such situations. If you are prone to these attacks and there is no spiritual or actual reason why they are occurring, then medication can be taken to keep that trigger from going off prematurely. It's really the trigger that needs fixing and not the panic system.

If you are a sufferer of panic attacks, be assured of one thing, you will not die or burst into flames. For the most part the body is designed to handle that release, and unless you have a weak heart or high blood pressure to start with, no harm will come. To stop them there is no quick cure, as for the most part we don't know what brings them on if no apparent danger is evident and no stressful situation has arisen. What we need to do is work on our trigger system and find out why it is faulty. Some people can feel them coming on, and if that be the case, we can go into counter mode with countering control. Things like prayer; getting away from large crowds or loud, noisy places; watching your breathing and focusing on what is really true and what is not. I would always have a scripture ready to recite. Second Timothy 1:7 always comes to mind and has helped me. *"For God hath not given us the spirit of fear; but of power, and of love, and of a sound mind."* We must practice talking to ourselves and talking ourselves out of this panic mode. Saying things like "There is no real reason to panic, God is with me, there is no danger, I will not die or self-destruct—I'm going to be okay, no one is going to kill or harm me—no present danger."

Panic is there for a reason. We need to make it our friend and not our enemy. When we learn to not be afraid of it but learn and know more about it, we can even be thankful that the Lord made us with such an emergency system. We then need to only ask for the Lord to help repair its discharge.

When Ending It All Appears So Appealing (Yes, Christians Think About Suicide)

After this Job opened his mouth, and cursed his day.
And Job spake, and said,
"Let the day perish wherein I was born, and the night in
which it was said, There is a man child conceived."

—Job 3:1–3

Today we begin a journey into the darkest place of all. That is that place of contemplating suicide. Though thinking about taking your own life is bad enough, what is also sad is how many Christians there are who don't thinks it is possible for a believer to even think of such a thing. If there is a taboo in Christian circles, there is certainly one in this area. Dear friend, before I move on with this chapter, I want to vent here a bit with the hopes that I don't offend anyone even though I probably will. Sometimes the worst people I have ever encountered are Christians themselves. If there is anything that is a liability to Christ's work, it is how we take His wondrous love, grace, and salvation and trample all over it by our pious self-righteous, hypocritical lives. Yes, I said it. Christians are sometimes the worst examples of Christ and do more damage to the Gospel than even an atheist can do. We are truly our own worst enemies. We judge others even though we have been forgiven of all. We live like the world and yet complain about the world that we really and secretly miss being a part of. We fight among ourselves over trivial things to the point that churches split over them. We are sneaky, nasty, and so far from where Christ longs for us to be. We dress, talk, and act like the world while claiming to be followers of Christ. We have our pet peeves of certain sins that we like to march and protest about yet feel no remorse for our own sins on lying, lusting, greed, pride, laziness, and inconsistency in what we say we believe. When it comes to things like depression and anxiety, we are so quick to point a finger and accuse a person of not having enough faith. What's worse is that all these traits come right down from our pastors and leaders. Every day another one bites the dust and falls. We say you need more faith while our own faith is far from perfect. We choose what we seem as important while tossing Christ's will and desires out the door. Sometimes I watch preachers on TV and at certain venues or online churches and say to myself, *If I was an unsaved person, this bozo is the last person I would turn to, and Christianity is the last place I would run.* Have you sat back and watched ourselves and then wonder why we are the laughingstock of the world and media. No, it is not because we are proclaiming the Word of God that we are attacked but because we are hypocrites and fools. I personally don't think that the average church service today is anything like Paul would have approved of. We have made church into a business and used the world's tricks to do it.

Okay, I am done with my rant, but I needed to set the stage for why things like depression and mental issues in the church are so stepped on and over while we claim to be beacons of love and understanding. It is like we are trying to hide the fact that we are sinners by pushing our dirty laundry out the door. Dear friend, when you become a child of God through faith in Jesus Christ, you don't stop being human. Sure some pastors and teachers on TV try to sell you that lie. They try to sell this vision of us becoming superheroes the minute we come to Christ. Well, just read your Bible and you will see that becoming a follower of God doesn't make one better than anyone else or exempt us from problems.

Depression is real, suicide is real, and shame on us if we are ashamed of our own people for not being able to part the seas the day after they are baptized in the Holy Spirit through believing in Christ. We fall, we are tempted, cut us, and we still bleed. I feel that the moment the church of Jesus Christ starts acting like Christ is the moment we will become real to the world and not a joke.

So let us begin this discussion on depression now and try to understand its varied dynamics, causes, and treatments. If you have lived, you have thought about not living. From the casual thoughts of "What's the point? I wish I was never born" to the all-out desire to end it all. Dear friend, I have been there, and if I was not, I could not honestly write about such a thing as suicide. I have been there all the way with death just seconds away. My first time was with a gun in my hand, bullets loaded and a note left for my family. I spent many hours lying in bed with tears trying to figure out the best way to take my life and then running through every scenario of the aftermath and what people would find and say. I planned on killing myself in a garage with exhaust fumes, to jumping off a roof, to driving my car off the side of a road. There was a time when it was all I could think about and focus on. I was sneaky, quiet, and deceptive. This wasn't a cry for help or to get noticed. It was a genuine desire to leave this life and be with the Lord. So those who know what I am talking about know that I know about this darkest demon of depression. See, depression has one goal in Satan's mind, and that is to get us to take our lives. It is Satan's favorite desire and will for humankind. If he could have a mass suicide, he would, which is why you find those cult mass suicides so often found around a corrupted Christianity or religious group.

Let us now go over suicide and what brings us to that place, how we can turn around from that place, and even how we can be blessed by that place. First off, if you are thinking, or have ever thought about taking your life, you are not insane or ready for the loony bin. If so, then Elijah, David, King Saul, Job, and so many great people of faith would also be ready for the loony bin. Maybe they didn't so much plan it but at the least thought of having had enough of this place. No, suicide is not so much the issue but why you are there.

Types of Suicide

There are two people that you run into in counseling, those who have thought about suicide and those who are planning it. If you have thought about it, it only makes you human without the answer God is trying to show you. If you have, or are planning it, then you have crossed over the line. Before I go further, let me just say this. If planning your demise is where you are at right now, well, please make this next lifesaving step, tell someone about it! Call 911 or a suicide hotline. Call your pastor or trusted friend.

Why Suicide?

Not unlike anxiety attacks, thoughts of suicide are a warning light. As panic attacks are a signal that something isn't working right, so are thoughts of taking your own life a signal that something is wrong. As in both cases the signal is mostly one from the Lord. Yes, I said that. Thoughts of suicide can sometimes be, and in most cases are, a signal from the Lord Himself that you need to listen up. Sure He probably was sending you signals a long time ago and the depression was the last stage of reaching you, but when that didn't work, He had to pull out all the stops and hit you with a sledgehammer. Suicidal thoughts are always for a purpose, but sometimes they can be fabricated. If that be the case, then you are not suicidal at all but looking for help, and it's the only way to get people to take notice. In my practice I had a young lady that holds the record for most attempted suicides. In the beginning we would make a big fuss, the police were called, prayers were said, hands were held, and long hours at her bedside watching over her. Yet it didn't take long for us to figure out that she never really wanted to take her life but that she just liked how important it made her feel. After years of this and lies after lies about things that never happened, it didn't take a brain surgeon to figure out the problem was not depression at all. She was just a young woman who liked being fussed over. Sure there was more to the story but to make a point—suicidal attempts or threats do not make one suicidal in all cases. Now as to other reasons for suicide, the list goes on and on. There is escape-based suicide, not so much for the intent to escape severe depression but to escape a self-erected catastrophe. Like in the case of a person who knows they are going to get caught for embezzling company funds, or a person who did a heinous crime like rape or had an affair. A person who lost all their money in the stock market or even a pastor or high official caught in a sexual sin such as a pedophile. These are reasons why some people attempt suicide, which by the way are the ones that usually go all the way to completion. But these are not depression-based suicides, so for the sake of wasted paper and trees, we will not cover them.

Another reason for suicidal attempts and thoughts are to threaten either a person or God. When we are at the end of our rope and the Lord doesn't seem to be listening, we illogically think that a suicide attempt or plan will get his attention. I actually did that in my first planned suicide, as I was sure the Lord would send down angels to my rescue. No. All He said to me was "Go home, you silly child, and stop this." I did, and soon after, I was out of my depression and serving the Lord like never before. In my two planned suicide attempts I never followed all the way through, nor was I brave enough to complete it. I never even had an attempted suicide, which simply means I was a coward, when being a coward is a good thing. Friends, it takes a lot of courage to take one's life, and most don't have it in them. Even as a Christian, the thoughts of heaven and our salvation quickly go through our minds. I remember thinking, *What if I am not saved, and I end up in hell.* Funny how odd our thoughts can be in such a time as that. I praise the Lord that fear kept me alive at that moment. Dear friend, we cannot threaten the Lord or trick Him into doing what we want. He controls all things and will not be intimidated. Does He want us to take our lives? Certainly not, but like all that man does to move the Lord, suicide must never be used as a pry bar.

Another reason we move to suicidal thoughts is pain, be it physical or mental. In this book we will focus on mental pain. Maybe it is being alone or the loss of a loved one or whatever drives you to it, it is all horrific. Mental pain is a silent scream that no one can hear but you, and of course the Lord. It is the worst kind of pain because there are few who will give you sympathy for it. Many times people actually believe you are faking it, and so pity is hard to come by. It is a pain that is multiplied each day by people telling you, "You don't look sick." How many times have I heard from depression sufferers who said that people were so surprised that they were depressed. Yes, depression, like functioning alcoholics, is easy to hide. Suicidal-leaning depression is like being buried alive and trapped in that coffin. You can bang all you want, but no one hears you. This extreme depression is being so tired of fighting to just simply get out of bed and go to work that it just doesn't seem worth it anymore. It is fighting things like daily anxiety and believing that there is no end in sight. You look at your life, you see others enjoying theirs, and you think to yourself, "If this is how I will live out my days, I would rather not live at all." You become tired of the promises, the false hopes, the breaking through of the sun for a few days, and then the discouragement of falling back into it again. It is for all of these reasons that people start to think of taking their lives. No, I am not endorsing it but trying to explain why people are driven to it. Unless you have been there, you do not know how powerful this force is. I know many people say that they would never take their lives, but I truly believe that given the right circumstance you just might. I'm sure King Saul never thought he would ever want his life ended as he was a mighty king and solider.

So the pain is real, as is the desire to end that pain. Pain at the end of the day is what we want to be gone. Ending our lives is not really the goal but simply, as I just said, ending the pain. This often makes me think of the horrors of hell, Can you imagine being in hell, in the worst suffering and agony and knowing that it will never be gone? You would even wish you could take your life, but it is already taken. Gives me chills just thinking about that. Anyway, back to this last chance ditch effort, God doesn't want it, you really don't want it, no one wants it, but the pain is real. Where do we go, what do we do, how can this be ended?

The Answer to Suicide

The answer to this question of leaving suicidal thoughts behind is found in logical thinking. Unfortunately logical thinking is not what we are doing when suicide is running through our minds, but praise the Lord. If Christ be in us, we can make the right choice and we can stop the madness. When the Bible says that "we can do all things through Christ that strengthens us," is it not also the strength that we need to make really hard choices? I know this to be true because that's what saved my life. I remember clearly one day, that day when it was very close to the end. I could not go on a moment longer in this place of tormenting, debilitating anxiety and depression. I had not eaten more than a morsel of food in over a month, and my pants were falling off me. I looked horrible, I was weak, and I had decided that I could go on no more. I decided to take a drive to think and plan out the logistics of my demise. While I was driving around, I pulled over to think, and while there I felt a compulsion to put the radio on. It was a Christian station, and the speaker was talking about, of all things, taking your life and what it leaves behind. He went on about our children and how they will never be the same. How the memory of you taking your life would most likely lead them to do the same one day. He went on and on about the pain of those left behind and the scars that we would be guilty for. Our children's lives would be forever tarnished. Wow, talk about the Lord interceding at the last minute. Dear friend, it was that pivotal moment that the Lord spoke to me through a radio show that was so directed at me that I knew it was of God. I also knew that if the Lord went through such efforts to reach me and keep me alive, He must know that my pain would soon leave. I decided that day to never, *ever,* entertain the thoughts of suicide no matter how bad things were. I could not have done it for myself. It was Christ in me and through me that helped me to do what I could never do alone.

In Closing

If you are at that dreadful place, if you are thinking those dreadful thoughts, if you have read all that I have just written and still feeling like you cannot go on, then I give you this advice: give up! Yes, you heard me. Give up fighting in your own strength and cry out to the Lord as I did. Cry out like Job and Elijah. The Lord will prove Himself. Of that there is no doubt. The Lord will not forsake you. Of that you must believe. Know that the pain will end, that the trial will be over and you will not have to live in this pain forever. These are not just words. These are not just words of a counselor or person who has never been where you are at. I have been there in every aspect of the agony. I know it is real, and I know how tired you are from fighting to hold on. If God was not real, then I would be dead and not writing these words to you today. He is real, and He loves you.

Hold on and, if anything, think about the words that the radio Bible teacher spoke to me that day. What of your family, friends, loved ones, coworkers, and even more, what of your testimony to a lost world? Also be afraid of taking that last breath and what will face you on the other side. Are you 100 percent sure of your salvation, your place in God's kingdom? What if you are not saved and you think you are? What if God is using this depression to draw you to Him for salvation because He knows you think you are but you are not? What if Satan has convinced you that you are saved by your church attendance and good deeds but you never really confessed Jesus as Lord? Dear friend, I would rather have you question your salvation at this point than to end your life not being completely sure. It could be a trick of the cloven-hoofed one. And if it be a trick, then ending your life now will not take you out of pain but enter you into a level of pain where there is no escape, no hope, no second chances. In hell you cannot die because you are already dead. The flames are real and the torment is everlasting and intense. It has no end, and in that place, you would wish to be back on earth again in your depression. I often think of the millions of people who ended their lives here as unbelievers and opened their eyes in the torments of hell. Talk about going from the frying pan into the fire. Am I trying to scare you? You bet I am, because I questioned my salvation, and it was enough to get me to make sure that I truly did know Christ as Lord. Suicide is the devil's trip wire, his bear trap, his crown jewel of victory. Don't let him get the satisfaction of laughing as you pass from this life into one far worse. Turn to Christ and seek Him out with all your heart. Make your salvation sure and confident, for in that confidence there is no need of escape but of rejoicing in peace. Of Christians getting depressed, and do they think about taking their lives, yes, they do—but even in salvation there is the unknown risk of disappointing the Lord. No one knows how the Lord will welcome us if we take our lives. Are you willing to take that chance? Now I am not suggesting that suicide is the unpardonable sin, nor does it send you to hell, but I, for one, don't want to be the test rat to prove it wrong or right. Eternity is way too long.

Why Doesn't the Evangelical World Understand This?

The heart of the wise is in the house of mourning; but the heart of fools is in the house of mirth.

—Ecclesiastes 7:4

Today we enter into the chapter that will most likely get under the skin of many Christians. A chapter about the major failing in the church today of dealing with those of us who struggle with what *they don't believe* we have. Before we begin this study, I want to share with you some studies and papers written about this so you don't think it is just me who is seeing this bigotry in the church.

Did you know that one in four households in your church is afraid to tell you this secret?
Check out this article by Carlene Hill Byron

How many families in your church have a loved one who struggles with mental health problems? That's kind of a trick question. People don't talk about mental health problems. You're more likely to hear them describe their child's condition as "something like autism," as the elder of one church we know says.

Or they might cover up entirely, as an elder's wife in another congregation did when her bipolar disorder swung into mania after childbirth,

The answer to the question is:

If your congregation is representative of the U.S. population, one in four households will struggle with someone's mental health problems over their lifetime. That's schizophrenia, bipolar disorder, obsessive compulsive disorder, disabling chronic depression, and various anxiety disorders.

Look at the faces seated around you this Sunday. Someone is probably hurting and probably afraid to tell you.

The least acceptable disability

A study where people ranked disabilities by their "acceptability" returned these results, in order, most acceptable: obvious physical disabilities, blindness, deafness, a jail record, learning disabilities, and alcoholism. Least acceptable: mental health problems.

People with mental health problems frighten us because when people become mentally ill, they become someone we don't know. That's what many people see when they look at those with mental health problems. It's hard to believe that people may behave in such unacceptable ways and not be in control of their behavior. Having a mental health problem is a lot like being on alcohol or drugs, without being able to stop. Medications "work" for about two-thirds of us. That means that a third of us can't ever get off the chemical ride that our brains produce. For those of us who can use medications, the side effects can be daunting. Many people become so frustrated with side effects that they stop taking medications. Only about half of us accept treatment. Even when we are treated, not everyone regains their status as a fully functioning adult.

What the Bible says

The Bible talks about mental illness, as well as physical illness. It describes a king who was made mentally ill until he would recognize the sovereignty of God (Daniel 4:29–34). It describes demonized men who lived among the tombs and terrorized everyone until Jesus set them free (Matthew 8:28–33). It also describes as demonized a young boy that most scholars today say had epilepsy (Matthew 17:15–18). Jesus delivered him too.

What does this tell us about illness?

First, that God is able to heal. Second, that some physical and mental illnesses are caused by demons. Third, that some mental illnesses are caused by sin. But are all mental illnesses caused by demons or sin, and is seeking God our sole resource for physical and mental healing?

Since the 1950s, we have usually sent church members with epilepsy to doctors for effective treatment with anti-convulsing drugs. In a similar way, we've learned that medicines can effectively treat many cases of mental illness. So if all mental illnesses were caused by demons and sin, then medicine would be exorcising demons and turning hearts to repentance. That is certainly untrue, for those are the works of the Holy Spirit. Instead, we now know that many mental illnesses are biological in origin, with environmental factors possibly triggering an existing genetic predisposition to the illness. Mental illnesses, just like epilepsy, are biological disorders of the brain.

Great article and very enlightening—kudos to Carlene Hill Byron. Dear friend, isn't it amazing how hearing facts instead of believing in opinions can be so liberating? It is sad that if we are told something long enough we will be begin to believe it even if it is not the truth. We will assume that if most people believe it and leaders teach it, it must be true. I once did a sermon called Lab Coat Theology, in which I wore a lab coat as I preached and held a clipboard instead of my Bible. I asked the people to be honest, and I asked them, "Now is what I say to you more believable simply because I appear more prone to be intelligent simply by wearing a lab coat?" They all said yes. Dear friend, if that be true, then people simply by virtue of their education, are, in our eyes, less likely to be wrong or even be in sin. We must stop being so impressed by people in power and start becoming people who look for scriptural truth instead. I don't care what a certain theologian said or how many pastors or churches believe it. If it be not in line with the Holy Writ, then it is wrong. I once had a debate with a young, godly man who had a great knowledge of scripture and recall. We were discussing a certain doctrine that he was trained in. He could not believe that I didn't believe this same doctrine, which in my mind was a complete manipulation of scripture. I remember him in great anger saying to me, "You mean to tell me that this famous theologian and that famous theologian are wrong and little old Pastor Scott is right?" I simply replied that "How do you know that they are right, is it impossible for man to be in error about the things of God?" See, when we begin to hold up mere mortals as infallible simply due to their celebrity status, are we not holding them up above God? Can a great man of God be right on everything else and wrong on this? Again, to say that some theologian is right about everything in the Bible is to imply that he is infallible. Now I don't claim to know everything—heck, I know very little—but I do know some things. To say that the crowd must be right and one lone solider is wrong is to fall into mob-rule mentality. It grinds my bones when the media, whether it is Christian or secular, comes out and endorses a pastor or evangelist. Recently in the news, a very famous and popular Christian author and pastor has been labeled "America's Pastor." How can this be, and how can we accept that? Well, we do when we let people tell us who is right and who is not. Psalm 118:8 is a scripture that I probably use too often, yet it seems so applicable to today's starstruck tendencies. Like when all of a sudden a movie star's opinion about politics and religion become more important than what the Bible says or even more important than what you and I say. With all that said, I would like to present to you another article from the news that brings to our table some more inconvenient truths. Please listen up.

Article August 30, 2013

Increase in adult suicides prompts call for greater prevention efforts.

With the most recent available data showing Minnesota having the highest rate of suicide in more than a decade, state officials are highlighting the importance of knowing suicide warning signs and that mental illnesses are treatable and suicides preventable. The Minnesota Department of Health (MDH) today released its most recent suicide data collected from 2011 death certificates. The data shows a 13 percent increase in the number of suicides, from 606 in 2010 to 684 suicides in 2011. Minnesota's suicide rate of 12.4 per 100,000 residents in 2011 was the highest since the early 1990s. Most of the increase in numbers from 2010 to 2011 is from men in their middle years, with the greatest increase in numbers for those 55–59 years of age. The suicide rate among seniors over 65 also increased in 2011 from a rate of 10.2 to 13.8 per 100,000. Youth suicides under 25 years of age saw a small increase from 5 per 100,000 to 5.7 per 100,000. "Today's news clarifies that we must do more to connect with those who are suffering and contemplating suicide," said Minnesota Commissioner of Health

Dr. Ed Ehlinger. "This is especially important because we know suicides are preventable. Most people who consider suicide do not kill themselves. They find hope and help." The 2011 figures follow Minnesota's long-term trends of steady suicide rates among youth and rising rates among adults 25 to 64. Minnesota's increase in adult suicides also mirrors a national trend. In May, the U.S. Centers for Disease Control and Prevention (CDC) reported that the annual, age-adjusted suicide rate among people aged 35–64 increased 28.4 percent, from 13.7 per 100,000 in 1999 to 17.6 per 100,000 in 2010. The CDC noted that while most suicide research and prevention efforts focus on youth and older adults, recent data underscore the need for prevention strategies serving adults aged 35–64. According to the CDC, prevention efforts are particularly important for baby boomers because of that generation's size, history of elevated suicide rates, and movement toward older adulthood, the period associated with the highest suicide rates. More research is needed to understand what is driving the increase among Minnesota adults. While some experts have suggested the recent economic downturn may be one contributing factor, suicide is complex. There are often multiple contributing factors such as mental illness, substance abuse, history of trauma and impulsive behavior. A persons' risk of suicide may increase with a painful loss, social isolation, feelings of hopelessness or being a burden to others, and not asking for help. The Adverse Childhood Experiences (ACE) study released by MDH this past winter found that more than half of all Minnesotans have had traumatic experiences early in life, and research has shown traumatic experiences early in life are associated with a higher rate of suicide attempts. Based on Minnesota's data, public health leaders are pushing to update and increase prevention activities with specific emphasis on high-risk groups such as middle-aged adults. To make progress in this area, MDH, DHS, and other state agencies are partnering with SAVE (Suicide Awareness Voices for Education) and other community-based agencies and advocacy groups to form the Minnesota Suicide Prevention Planning Task Force. Task force responsibilities will include updating the state's 2007 suicide prevention plan to incorporate new strategies targeting high- risk groups such as adults, as well as recommendations from the National Strategy for Suicide Prevention. As the new plan is developed, the task force will leverage existing suicide prevention efforts such as the DHS mental health and crisis services, DHS and private crisis phone lines, the TXT4Life initiative, and MDH and local community suicide prevention efforts. (End of Article)

I could go on and on with article after article, research statistics after research statistics, and they would all say the same thing: depression and emotional issues are all around us and are here to stay in every demographic of our society, and to say that the only place where it is not found is in the church is complete pride and bigotry, pure and simple. We are human, and so we all share the same DNA pool. Christ came to save the lost from sin but not to make us sinless or never sick with pain or problems. As sinners saved by grace, we will always be sinners. As people born into a sinful, fallen world, we will always be people living in a sinful, fallen world. As long as we are alive on planet Earth, we are susceptible to all of its corruptions. Do Christians get cancer, diabetes, and heart disease? Do our homes get broken into, and do our loved ones die? To think that being in Christ is to never be sick or never able to catch a cold is foolishness. Germs are out there, people get sick, and pain is a part of it. Are not children born into Christian families born with birth defects, sickness, and mutation? Does a person who has down syndrome become healed when they come to Christ? If a person who is in Christ loses their job do to the economy or loses their home due to a tornado, are they not susceptible to depression? What of our wonderful soldiers who had to face the horrors of war and come home with PTSD, are they any less a Christian or has Christ somehow failed them? Dear friend, I believe in divine healing as according to the Lord's will, but I also know that many times the Lord does not heal. If that were not true, then every Christian would never be sick or have any physical or mental / emotional issues. For those who want to simply say that God only heals us through supernatural healing is to say that God only fixes a blocked artery through prayer. I don't know about you, but I visit many Bible-believing Christians in hospitals, those who we have prayed over earnestly and many of them are healed through the doctor's hand and medications. Let us please stop the taboos about mental and emotional issues in the church. If we have them, then the Lord knows about it and has prepared a means to deal with them. What I urge you to do is to speak up at your local church. Let us educate our leaders and laypeople. If we don't through pride of being found out, then aren't we caring more about our own pain instead of maybe standing up for those who are suffering and feeling ashamed to speak of their pain? Let us break the silence. Let us speak up for those who cannot speak for themselves. We do it for the unborn killed in abortions, so why should we not do it for those who can't speak for themselves due to emotional turmoil? Let us also not forget Scripture and what the Lord says about joy and pain. Joy isn't always the goal, dear friend, as sometimes the Lord chooses to have us go through times of pain and sorrow. I don't know a Christian who has not. In Ecclesiastes 7:4 a powerful statement is made. *"The heart of the wise is in the house of mourning; but the heart of fools is in the house of mirth."* To live only to be happy places you in a place where you can never hear the deep counsels of God. If the Lord chooses to use depression and anxiety to reach us with the deep things of Himself, then who are we to say that they don't exist and should not exist in the heart of a child of God? Break the silence today!

Friends, Family, and Spiritual Counselors a Trinity of Ignorance?

"Blessed is the man that walketh not in the counsel of the ungodly, nor standeth in the way of sinners, nor sitteth in the seat of the scornful."

—Psalm 1:1

How can so many people that mean so well and care so much about me be so far off when they try to counsel and comfort me? I remember my first bout with depression and anxiety. I was a deacon in my church and really active. Suddenly out of the blue I am hit with this sledgehammer of emotional pain. In the beginning I tried to just work through it and keep it from family and friends and certainly from my church family. When it became to be unbearable, I had to let my family know. They all surrounded me with love and compassion, yet for the most part they had zero knowledge of anything like this. If I had the flu, they would bring me hot soup; if recovering from a broken leg, they might come over and help me around the house; but of emotional trauma, they were clueless. My wife was the greatest help, but even there we were entering uncharted waters. It also became a very private thing, and one we kept hush-hush. There is no other way to look at it but that we were ashamed and embarrassed. Yes, it was prideful, and we were in sin, but we couldn't help this feeling that this issue is not allowed or expected in a Christian. As time went on, I became worse, and we were at a loss. Since there was no real help in the Christian world, we had to dabble in the secular world. I went from counselor to counselor. One lady that I saw had me talking about sex and my relationship with my mother as a child. I would leave there and wonder what any of that had to do with my depression issues. There was no prayer, no talking about God, no scriptures. Even the so-called Christian counselors that I went to did not mention God or scriptures for the most part. They just put a fish symbol on their business card and called themselves Christian. By the way, it was through those days that the Lord spoke to my heart about the need for a true Christian counseling body. After things got better, I began going to school and earned my master's in Christian counseling. But back to my search for help, it came time that I had to let more people know about my problem. This happened against my will one Sunday when I was down in the nursery hiding because I couldn't stop crying. Some lady from church saw me and knew something was wrong. Before I knew it the secret was out, and honestly I didn't care anymore. I was tired of hiding, and to some degree it was a relief to let my guard down. Now it was okay for awhile, but then when word got out, the cards and letters started coming in. People sent me so many books on my issues, but all were secular. I received wonderful uplifting cards and letters and even got a visit by a few elders and the pastor. People sent me cassette study programs on how to beat anxiety and depression, which by the way only made me worse. People would pray over me and for me, and I would cry. Gee, I cried a lot and just complained to everyone that came. Going back to church every Sunday was hard, because now I had to face the greeting line of people asking me the same questions over and over again. "How are you feeling, are you better, I am praying for you, and what can I do for you?" After a while it was downright humiliating, and I became angry and annoyed at the constant questioning. Then came the next phase, the phase when people get tired of asking and the visits become less and less. It is one thing to be sick for a few weeks, but when a year goes by and

I am still not well, people begin to talk. People do what sinners do. They begin to speculate and gossip: "Maybe Scott is involved in some sin, maybe the Lord is punishing him, and maybe he is never going to be okay and will have to be placed in the hospital." It then becomes "Poor Scott," and worse, "Maybe he is just faking it to get attention." Of dumb things to say to a person suffering from emotional issues, here are a few that I would get: "Just snap out of it, be happy, you have so much, Jesus loves you and has a wonderful plan for you, just be happy. Just try to see the good in life, just try to be happy." I tell you, I would become secretly enraged at some of those comments, and after that season passed, I just started lying. "I'm fine, doing good, don't worry about me, I'm trusting in the Lord."

But, dear friend, I was not getting better. Instead I was slipping deeper and deeper into the darkness. I just couldn't go on any longer as every day and week and month became something to dread. The point that I make is this. No one really knew what to do because the church is not equipped for this. As to medication it was unheard of and foolish to even consider. Counselor after counselor, phone conversations with dear brothers and sisters in Christ, reading my Bible, devotions, and praying—it all did nothing for me. I was dying, and I knew I was, and on one January day with tears in my eyes and gun in my hand, I tried to make one last phone call to my pastor, but for some reason, I couldn't reach him. I couldn't reach anyone, and so I drove and drove crying and planning out how this would all go down. That morning I lied to my wife and told her I had a meeting with the pastor and instead slipped a note into her pocketbook saying good-bye. I also got on my knees and hugged my two little boys, told them I loved them and to take care of mommy 'cause Daddy is going to be with Jesus. They couldn't understand as they were too little, but it was important that I said good-bye. Back in my car I drove to the local beach and just sat there as the waves crashed. I tried to find a reason to keep living as I fumbled through my Bible. I found none, as the Bible seemed silent that day. I took it and tossed it, waiting for angels to sweep me away. I told the Lord that this was it, and so He better stop me. He did by only speaking a few words into my ears: "Go home, you silly child of mine, go home to your wife and family." I did and told my wife what happened. I told her how bad I really was and that I didn't know what to do. We called a family meeting and waited for my mom and dad to arrive. We all sat down, and I explained that I couldn't work anymore and needed help. See what I really wanted was for them to sweep me off my feet and bring me home into their loving arms and have them make it all better. To my shock and surprise they said, "We are sorry, but we don't know what to do either, and we cannot help you. You need to keep working and moving on."

Dear friend, it was at this point that there were no other option on the table. I had no idea what to do. I was completely alone and lost with no one knowing what to do. It was not until that night that my dear sister, a powerful Christian, called from California and said these words, "Brother, I love you, but you need to go on medication." To that I said, "No way, if I be healed, it would be God that is healing me." Then she hit me with the medications we all take for high blood pressure and high cholesterol. She talked me into it, but it was on a winter's night with snow coming down. If I was going to get medication, I would have to see the only doctor that I knew, which was our family doctor. He was a very nice man an old country doctor type. My wife called him, and he drove out in the snow and met me at his office. He prescribed me a mild antidepression medication, and we filled it that night. I remember looking at that pill for a long time, afraid to place it in my mouth. After a while my wife became annoyed and said, "Please take it, babe, I don't know what else to do for you, and I don't want to lose you." I took the pill that night, and after a few months and some changes in medication that fit me better, I began to heal. I began to be able to pray again, read the Bible, and hear from the Lord. Then one might I was woken up at about 3:00 a.m. with a scripture the Lord had placed in my mind. It was Habakkuk 1:1–5. It was that night that the Lord spoke to me and told me that what He has planned for me is so wonderful that If He was to tell me right then, I would not be able to even believe it. That day was the beginning of my healing and new beginnings. It was after that day that I went back to school, gained multiple degrees, and wrote and published my first book, *Spiritual Living in a Sexual World*, and was soon called to be a pastor. In the meantime, I was running my counseling practice part time, which would eventually become full time. It was from that day that I would be filled with enough faith to quit my high-paying cushy job with a parking spot by the front door with my name on it. The Lord told me to start searching for a church to pastor. I found one only three thousand miles away. I soon sold my home and most of my possessions—quit my wonderful job with health insurance, perks retirement, college for my kids, and job security—and in a short time I was driving with my entire family and our cat Frisky all the way to California from New York. All this right in the middle of winter, to a church that could not afford to pay me and a ministry where I would have to work full-time doing construction labor work. It was scary and humbling, but what an Abraham moment of faith testing. The rest is history as so many, many things transpired and so bold I became in my faith—yes, even a person with extreme anxiety—which is where Philippians 4:13 came in. It would be fifteen years later that I would have my second bout with anxiety/depression, but that too would become a catalyst for great blessings that would follow. Also, I want you to know that as I write about these painful times in my life, it cannot help but bring up those old pains. As I write each word and remember those days, those pains become new and fresh in my mind. If I could be writing this in my own blood, I would, and in a way I feel like I am. Those pains and your pains do leave scars, and though we can pull nails out of a board, we still must leave holes behind. These pains will be hard to forget, and maybe they shouldn't, just as we shouldn't forget the pain that Jesus went through for us.

Dear friend, though your friends and family might not understand your pain, remember that the Lord Most High does. Why does He let us suffer so sometimes? I do not know, but I do know He gets the job done in making us see what we can be when we lay flat out in faith before Him. And not just during the easy times, but more importantly in the hardest times where faith is so hard to come by. God does change and transform. Just be willing to be faithful and hold on just a little longer. As to our loved ones, friends and family understand that they don't and can never understand something that they have never experienced. Just as I am a man can never know what it is like to give birth, so it is with our loved ones. As well meaning as they are, they can only comfort through ignorance. Be grateful if you have them, and if you don't, don't worry about that either because they're not much help anyway.

Ashamed to Be So Weak
(I Shouldn't Need Medication, Right?)

"Not by might, nor by power, but by my spirit,
saith the LORD of hosts."

—Zechariah 4:6

One of the hardest parts of being a Christian, and dealing with emotional issues is that of feeling like a failure. To be a follower of Christ and yet feel so weak and afraid can quickly lead one to even challenge their own salvation. We begin to look at other Christians and wonder what they have that we don't. In time, if we let him, Satan can really do a number on our self-worth. That is why I am writing chapter 8, a chapter that is going to take a lot of time to get through, but one that is oh so needed. Like I have shared with you before, my battle with depression and anxiety really left me feeling like the bottom of the spiritual barrel. Comparing me to others became a dangerous game, and one that left me angry, bitter, and jealous, and in case you didn't notice, those are all sins. What's wrong with being in sin is that we also place ourselves in a position where God is separated from us. Not that we have lost our salvation, but that we have lost our connection to the one who has saved us. Now before I go into the taboo of taboos, medications and the child of God, I first want to spend some time on pointing out how common it is for people of faith to have emotional issues. Take Job, for example, he complained, became depressed, and in time was wishing he was never born. Moses had the problem of feeling inadequate for the tasks ahead and actually thought that God made a bad choice in choosing him. We can look also at Timothy who had a problem with fear. Jehoshaphat had some issues with anxiety. Elijah has a problem with depression, which interestingly was right after a time of great success. Isaiah had a problem with guilt, and Jeremiah, sometimes called the weeping prophet, had the problem of doubt. The book of Jeremiah paints a picture of this man who had deep inner struggles.

He was plagued by feelings of being not up to the job (no self-confidence), filled with depression, doubt, and despair. He lamented about the betrayal of his friends and family, Jeremiah 11:18. He wondered and questioned the purpose of his life and ministry, Jeremiah 15:10–20. He was impatient with God for taking so long to answer him, Jeremiah 17:12–18. He yelled at and cried to God and accused God of deceiving him, Jeremiah 20:7. And Like many of us, he cursed the day he was even born, Jeremiah 20:14–18. What Jeremiah did, is what we all do. We listen to the lies of Satan: "You are not worth anything, you are a failure, God cannot use you, and you need to take your own life and then all will be well." One thing you will find in common in all of these biblical peoples lives and your own, is that (1) *they focused on themselves*, (2) *they complained to God*, (3) *God used their pain for the end result*, and (4) *GOD delivered them.*

Now as we move closer to how they and we are delivered from depression and anxiety, let us also take careful note of what means the Lord chooses to do so. What's interesting is how different the means are. I love when Jesus was performing His healing ministry on earth and how He made a point to not use the same method for each person or situation. Sometimes He just said, "*Be healed.*" Sometimes He placed mud and spat on a person's eyes. Sometimes He placed His fingers in a person's ears. The point is that, regarding healing throughout the entire Bible, God can just heal on the spot, but at other times He is creative on how

He does the healing. Is it God that ultimately heals? The point I would like to make throughout this chapter is yes, God heals, but He does so through elements of His choosing. Dear friend, when we are off center and need to be right sided up. The Lord is the master parbuckler, and the pulleys and levers that He uses are of His choosing. Now in case you don't know what parbuckling is, it's a term used by those of the nautical nature. Seamen and sailors know it well as when a great ship has capsized and needs to be righted. This procedure requires great rigging, pulleys, massive counterweights, and many varied devices to right such massive ships. In our life, though the Lord has the power to heal, He also has the wisdom to know what pulleys, counterweights, and rigging will get the job done best. Let us not limit how the Lord heals to what we decide is the best method. Is not He the master physician, and then would He not know the best treatment to give?

I think we are all familiar with Proverbs 3:5–8, which reads; *"Trust in the LORD with all thine heart; and lean not unto thine own understanding. In all thy ways acknowledge Him, and He shall direct thy paths. Be not wise in thine own eyes: fear the LORD, and depart from evil. It shall be health to thy navel, and marrow to thy bones."* Do not these scriptures clearly state that the Lord decides what's best for us and that we should not be telling Him how He should heal us?

In 2 Peter 1:3 we see this picture even better: *"According as His divine power hath given unto us all things that pertain unto life and godliness, through the knowledge of Him that hath called us to glory and virtue."* Friend, the Lord has provided all things for us as a people to live. Did He not make air for us to breathe and water for us to drink? What if we were to say, "No, I will trust in the Lord for my thirst and for my breathing," and then refuse to drink water and breathe air, would we not then die? Do we not see the foolishness of refusing all means in which the Lord heals and sustains us? Do we not take herbs and vitamins to keep us healthy? Do we not drink caffeine to wake up and give us a jolt as well as eat chocolate for its boost to our moods? In the great states of Oregon and Washington, the rainy season is so long and heavy that depression is a big issue. Because of that reason many people keep a bowl for of chocolate on the kitchen table to raise their moods. Is that sin then to eat such things that the Lord made to work with our bodies so well? Did not Paul tell Timothy to *take a little wine for thy stomach's sake* when no other medications were yet invented or discovered? In James 1:17 it says a few other things that we might want to consider in regard to the Lord using *anything and all things* for our good. *"Every good gift and every perfect gift is from above, and cometh down from the Father of lights, with whom is no variableness, neither shadow of turning"* (James 1:17). When I couldn't gather the strength to even live another day, medication and what the Lord allowed it to do for me sure seemed like a gift from God.

Since when are medications for emotional issues sinful yet medications for physical issues not? Dear friend, I will defend this issue with all of my heart, and I will take whatever heat I get for standing my ground. I am so angered at the hypocrisy of Christians when it comes to this issue of medications. I can say this with full confidence for one strong reason—I would be dead if I didn't use medications back when depression almost claimed my life. If they be sinful, then let me be cursed, but that's not what I see. I saw only a ray of sunshine when nothing else would work. I had to swallow my pride and trust in the Lord in a new way, but I am persuaded with every fiber of my being that it was of the Lord. Now let me make this perfectly clear as I know I will be misquoted on this issue. "I am *not* advocating medication at every single encounter and problem with depression and other emotional ailments." No, they are my last resort, for the most part with counseling, and I do not even like to bring them up unless I feel it would be beneficial. Yet sometimes I do see them as a first resort when I meet with a mature Christian who has exhausted every avenue already of the spiritual kind and they come to me at the end of their rope. When I tell them about medication and how a Christian can benefit by it, their eyes light up and hope is restored. That look on their faces is one I cherish as a sigh of relief comes over them. For so long many of them suffered in the agony of depression and have been ashamed to even think about medications, for they know how the "Christian" world will jump on them faster than flies on manure. What is amazing is how shocked they are that a pastor and Christian counselor would even suggest it. They will say things like, "But my pastor or Christians friends said that if I only had more faith, God would heal me and that God would never use medications as it shows no faith." Oh, does that boil my blood as I would like to tell these (friends of Job) advisors to not take their pain medications after a surgery or even after a tooth removal. Sure it is easy to claim faith when you are not sitting in the fire. To all of these highbrows of ignorance, I say this, "Walk a mile in my shoes before you accuse."

Dear friend, what if the faith that the Lord is looking for is the faith to trust Him in wherever and however He leads you. Also, please understand this, medications alone and faith in them is not the answer. Did you just hear what I said? Trusting in the medications is like trusting in money or even in a doctor, and that is not the answer. It is trusting and believing that God can use these things to do His healing. I know this because I have learned it. In my life on and off medications I found that they only worked when the Lord allowed them to. Meaning that when I began to feel better and then started to praise these medications, I was then forgetting who made them work. Right away they would stop working and I would wonder what happened. Once I started to understand that God must receive the praise and glory all the time, and then the Lord again allowed them to work. That's also how I knew it was the Lord using these medications for my benefit. Dear friend, I dare not tell you how many people sitting in the pews every Sunday are on medication for depression and anxiety. The answer would shock you, as well as how many pastors and elders, and even Christian counselors, are on them. Can they be abused, and misprescribed? You bet and they often are. I will also add that there must be something behind this massive increase of medication usage in the church and world, but until we can pinpoint it and repair it, we need to accept the Lord's present aid and benefit from them. Some say it is because of all the chemicals in all the cleaners, foods, and drinks we use that are messing up the wiring of our brains, maybe so. But again until we can get rid of the cause, we need to keep the medication option open. To clear up one more thing, I wish to clarify what medications I am not talking about. I am not talking about the abuse of the tranquilizing types of medications out there mostly for anxiety issues. These are abused so much that they have become almost a street drug. Being in a drunken state is never what the Lord would want. We are to be filled with the Spirit, not drunk with stimulants and depressants. So please let us be careful when we jump into the medication remedy. There is always more to the story and much more counseling and growing in Christ to be had. Medications can be a stopgap measure until we find the root cause of our pain, or they might be needed for the long haul. In most cases this approach has been the best and with the most success.

How They Work

Now I am not a pharmaceutical chemist, but I will throw out to you in layman's understanding how the (good) antidepressants work. First off, we must understand that our brains are filled and controlled by chemicals and electric signals. The brain is a masterful supercomputer, yet it does get its viruses and glitches. That is why not all emotional issues in a Christian are of the spiritual type, but some are actually of the chemical type. Chemical imbalances are not a catchphrase, but an actual condition of sorts. Take serotonin in our brain. It is a complex amine found in blood and the brain. It constricts the blood vessels and contracts smooth muscle tissues, and it is also an important neurotransmitter and hormone. Serotonin concentrates in certain brain areas, especially the midbrain and hypothalamus. Some cases of depression are apparently caused by reduced amounts or activity of serotonin in the brain. Many antidepressants counteract that condition, which is why they are used. They do work, but with any type of medication there is always the risk of overuse and side effects. The point I make here is we cannot discount the chemical and electrical makeup of the brain, and if these areas are weak or lacking, then why can't a medication designed to repair these weakness be used? And if maybe our depression is caused by environmental changes in our world, water and food supply, then why can't the Lord come up with something to combat the present world we live in? Throughout history, when a plague would hit mankind, it always seemed like the Lord gave man wisdom to find some drug to subdue it. Remember where penicillin comes from, friends? Did not God and does not God have all around us the cures for our sickness if we but look for them in His creation? And if there be those found to heal physical sickness, then why not emotional sickness?

For How Long?

One question we often hear is in regard to the duration of medications. Again I am not a doctor or chemist, but in my practice and personal experience, I have found the answer to be varied. Some people can take them for a year and then once back to normal they can be weaned off them by their doctor or mental health-care professional. Yet some people might have to take them for the rest of their life. Either way I do not think we should make a bigger deal out of it than needs be. Sure a life on no medications of any kind is always best. But if we have high blood pressure when we turn fifty, do we say to the doctor who prescribes the medications, "How soon can I get off these?" Sometimes you can, by diet and weight loss, but other times you can't, as in the case of severe diabetes. If we are to claim our great faith in the Lord and our unquestioning trust, then let's leave the "how longs" up to Him.

Aren't Medications Bad for You?

This question and topic always raises eyebrows as the world, especially the Christian world, has already made up their minds. Take for instance the recent news about mass shootings. Every time there is a mass shooting, two things are brought up, gun control and people on medication. Of the gun debate I won't get into that, but of the medication debate I certainly will. I read a recent article that states how medications cause mass shootings and suicides. They will start off by listing a shooting and also listing what antidepressant that shooter or violent person was on. Now if you're a person in need of medication or on some right now, you might look and say, "Hey, I am on that medication, will I become a mass killer?" Dear friend, please hear me out, because this is where the world digs in a pile of debris looking for what they desire to find. Just as the gun control advocates are looking for evidence for their case, so are the bigots of no medication for Christians suffering with emotional issues. What they don't tell you is how many people are taking medications and have not killed anyone lately. What they don't tell you is why the shooters took the medications in the first place and how high of a dose they were taking. What they don't tell you are how there are millions upon millions of people who are living happy, healthy lives due to their medications. If that were not so, then every person taking medications would be shooting people and taking their lives. To debunk this perversion and get the facts out, let's first draw some comparisons. Number one, taking too high a dose of any medication can lead to side effects. If you have heard those commercials for the various types of medications out there from heartburn to ED medications, you will also notice how they run quickly down the list of possible side effects. They list bleeding from every orifice in your body to sudden death. Yes, medications can have many side effects. The medication I was taking for high cholesterol is so dangerous that blood work was done every month to make sure my liver and kidneys weren't shutting down.

I had to look at the two sides of the spectrum: death now versus death later. Yeah, it's a crazy world out there, and if we choose or could even choose to be on nothing, it would surely be great, but I don't know many people who don't take anything at all. Plus, we all know the people like I know who hate any type of medication for anything, be it a flu vaccination to an antibiotic, so they take every vitamin and herbal powder known to man and are sick all the time. Now of the high dose question again, why were those shooters taking such a high dose? Did they go to their doctor for simple depression and anxiety, or did they go because they were borderline delusional with episodes of hearing voices and violent, aggressive outbursts? Please understand that this book is dealing with mostly depression and anxiety. We are not talking about way-out multiple personality disorders. Sad to say, many doctors in the mental health care field do overprescribe medications to subdue these extreme behemoths, but that's not what we are trying to correct here in the case of our target of mental health, and there are exceptions to the rule. Case in point, I do have someone that I have counseled for years, and she is probably on the most medications I have ever seen anyone on and still walking the streets. Yet she is a child of God and loves the Lord Jesus Christ with all of her heart. She does have a cocktail full of emotional issues, but without her medications, she could not live in society. I am happy to say that through Jesus Christ she is doing wonderfully and producing much. She is completely on her own and raising a child with great success. She leads people to the Lord and faithfully attends church. What of her and people like her, are they monsters, and should they be taken off their medications if they are working so well? Believe me, this person tried over and over again to get off these medications but simply cannot. She is praising the Lord today for finding the right doctor who prescribed the right medications in the right proportions. Listen, I am not on the payroll for the medication company, nor do I want anyone on medication if they don't need them. What I am asking for is an honest look at those who can benefit from them to serve Christ with a peaceful heart, free from judgment from the Christian community. My concern is that there is a person out there who is in real need of some help from medications and yet they won't take them because of all the stigma that goes along with them. Medication can help some, and yet some they can't. Medications do have side effects but always based on the individual and the particular circumstances. I have had Christians on medications that simply did not work and they were pulled off immediately. They ended up just needing really good and solid Christian counseling. Medications are not always the answer, nor are they a monster. This is why it is important to find a good doctor who really knows their stuff, one who is nonaggressive with his prescribing methods but instead reluctant. It is that type of mental health care provider who won't just try to mask the problem but find it and then go aggressively after that one particular area. One who is willing to incorporate counseling, prayer, and medications, but only if needed. In most cases I have found that very few medications are needed if at all. In my struggles I was always prescribed the smallest doses possible as my body just could not take anything more than a child's level of medication. That's just me, and some might do better on more, but to call all medications and people on them monsters in the making is to slaughter a complete demographic of people for the actions of a few. It is like when a car has a weakness in one area and a few accidents are caused, immediately the world goes after the manufacturer and all of those models are taken off the market just to make a few people happy. It is like putting out a candle with a fire hose where a tiny blow of our mouths could take care of it. Let's open our ears and our eyes that we may see where the truth truly lies and then carefully make our choices. Again I do not advocate or discourage medications in all or some cases but ask that we all have a clear, open mind. If we don't, we might find ourselves in a place of being a complete activist opposed to medication only to find out that our child ends up needing them. What then would you do? Would you be like the cults out there who keep medications, surgeries, and blood transfusions away from their child only to see them die? As the Scriptures so perfectly point out, "Be quick to hear and slow to speak." That is why the Lord gave us two ears but only one mouth.

Aren't Medications Really Cheating as They Are a Synthetic Happy Pill?

This question here is another one of my pet peeves. So many people including myself at one time assumed that medications for emotional issues are somehow a way of cheating in regard to faith in God because they fabricate a phony happiness. This again is an area where ignorance reigns supreme. Dear friend, if there was a happy pill, everyone on planet Earth would be killing for it. If you think that any type of antidepressant makes you happy, you are sadly mistaken. Let's be perfectly clear here. Happiness is found in only one place, and that is in Jesus Christ. There is no peace or, should I say, real peace anywhere else. Money can give you temporary peace, but when the money goes, so goes the peace. Sex, drugs, and rock 'n' roll can give you peace, but as we see in the life of celebrities, it is short-lived and only leads to depression. No, happiness is not found anywhere, but in a living saving relationship with Jesus Christ. As to medications making you happy, they do no such thing, nor could there be a pill that does. Take for example this scenario, you just lost your wife and kids in a horrible car accident or maybe your mother or father. Maybe you have lost all of your money due to a failed business. Do you think that any antidepressant could bring joy to that situation? For it to do so, it would have to be able to create an alternate reality and for the exception of taking LSD or some street narcotic, it's just impossible, nor is it what antidepressants are designed to do. See, medications for depression and anxiety don't replace thought and emotion, nor can they alter it. No, they simply elevate or adjust the amount of chemicals that are supposed to be in your brain back to normal levels. If you are sad because your car was just stolen, trust me, you will still be sad even on medication. Antidepressants are not even a good term to use as they don't stop you from being depressed by making you happy, but help your mind to function in a normal state. They simply make things equal to those around you so you have a level playing field when your field has been plagued by mud and rain. Mental traction is equalized but never tranquilized, or at least it shouldn't be. If a person is trying to find happiness, they can take all the medications they choose, but it will not work, which is actually why you end up with people going off the deep end. Also, taking medication does not leave you in a state of euphoria all day laughing and out of your mind. Trust me, I know, as when I took medication I never felt like that. In fact, when given the right dose, you shouldn't feel anything at all but simply normal again. If anything, feeling normal again does make you happy, so yes, you just might smile again when you haven't in many years. A while back I took on one of my most disturbing cases, which involved a thirteen-year-old boy. This boy came from a wonderful family, confessed to be Christians, and attended church regularly. The problem was that this young boy was horribly depressed and suffering with anxiety. He was a mild cutter, brilliant, and yet introverted to some degree. I counseled him for a while but realized prayer and Christian counseling was not enough. When I suggested medication, he and his family refused, and so I backed away. I instead referred him to an associate of mine, and for a while he seemed to be doing well. Yet the next thing I found out is that he was committed to a hospital for cutting, self-inflicted punching to his face, and thoughts of suicide. He is now on medication, but in my opinion much too late. My point is this, we are so appalled at the idea of ourselves or our child on any type of medication that we will withhold it due to pride and ignorance until it is too late. Like I have said before, medication when used properly and sparingly can help us from falling too deep into that pit. If we wait too long, we can fall so deep into that pit that we simply can't get out. I liken medication to a rope ladder thrown down to us in that hole where prayer and reading God's Word is no longer possible. How can I say such a thing? I was in that hole, and I wanted not my Bible or prayer any longer. All I wanted was to die and be freed from the pain. Medication can be, not *must be*, but can be that rope ladder. So again, medications are not happy pills but are more like a pacemaker placed on a weak heart. Just as a pacemaker on a heart simply allows the heart to work as it was meant to, so does medications allow our brains to function as they were made to. I pray that this point on medication and the Christian has been made. Faith in God again is trusting Him in whatever means He chooses to use.

Those Who Want Medication Too Soon

Another thought and discussion on medications and the child of God, I would like to warn you of is the flip side. That is the person who is too quick to want medications. Believe it or not, it is less common, but there are those who say, "Give me medications and let them fix all the problems." Dear friend and fellow sufferer, this is not a good sign or desire, nor can any medication fix any problem really, but simply help you in finding those answers on your own. Any person who wants medications as their first line of attack might be one who is not willing to trust the Lord first to see if He is even leading in that area. Sure we all want to feel better as soon as we can, but trusting too much in the medications, as I have shared before, is actually diminishing faith in the Lord. Yes, the medications can help and heal, but again only if the Lord chooses to use that route. I have met a few that wanted medication right off the bat, which was a hint to me that they might not even be willing to try Christ. As I have spoken of much in this book, there is going to be a struggle sometimes, and there is going to be a fight. Sometimes the Lord is going to want us to get out of bed on our own and get that first leg on the floor. Many times even those medications won't help you get out of that bed either. Your will and desire may still be necessary. As we look through the scriptures, we see clearly that the Lord often lets His dear ones fight for life and liberty simply by having them wait on His timing. Now this might sound partly like a contradiction to some of what I have stated elsewhere, but it is not. I am simply stating that wanting to be spared labor is not always of God. We are to sweat sometimes, and strive. We are to push ourselves and again focus on just getting that one leg out of bed and that one foot on the floor. Medication is a tool, and it can only be used well if the master mechanic is allowed to decide when or if that tool is needed at all. It is His call, not ours, for this you can be certain. So yes, medications are a tool, and they can save a life way off track, but that doesn't mean they should always be ran to. One reason I warn you of this is the fact that taking medications when you don't need them places you in a position of having a drug in your system that can have side effects and also the problem of being very difficult to get off of. In a perfect world, no medication of any kind, for any reason, is the best place to be but that's not always possible. Think and pray very hard about what road you choose. Make sure you are giving your health care provider the proper information about yourself so they can make an educated diagnosis in your particular case. I guess what I am trying to say is this. "Proceed with caution."

One Last Bit of Information to Leave You Confused

Dear friend and fellow sufferer, I have spoken much about depression and anxiety as that's what this book is about. I have spoken about the possible causes for such an epidemic to even exist today. I have tried to neither be pro or against medications and have explained why in some cases they may help, but—and I say a big *but* here—there is something that is an inconvenient truth about medication and this present age that is unlike any other. To some it might seem like bad news and to others good news, but regardless, it is something that I have recently learned and a truth that is well worth thinking about. In an article written by Carlene Byron, a noted author on this quest for mental health in this present age of the church, she writes about some factors worth considering plus a warning about medications. She speaks of the USA in particular and what it has caused to happen to our culture, which has made it a more mentally unstable culture than most.

Social environment. Westerners live in much more isolation now than at any time in human history. So much so that when one person of my acquaintance sought to volunteer with Mother Teresa, she told him to return to the United States, because in the United States was a "poverty of loneliness" unequaled in the world. We have abandoned our extended families and so are "free" to live whatever life we please, but also lack both the support (financial and emotional) these extended families offer and the understanding provided by people who know our heritage in multiple generations. It was not until after my mother's death, when notifying relatives, that I learned (at age 56) that she had been proud of me: she had been so committed to treat all her children "equally" that she had not treated us each as our specific abilities and interests deserved. Living in closer community with relatives it would have been more likely that I'd have learned that many years before. In addition to this isolation from family, our constant migration impoverishes us from connection with familiar community. The Body cannot be the Body when no one knows anyone and no small group "formula" designed to create intimacy in 18 months can achieve it. I truly believe that most depression and anxiety is rooted here, in our separation from the Body of Christ and the family of God. While it is true that God's love casts out all fear, we most often receive God's love through members of God's Body as they are fitted together perfectly, with Christ as the cornerstone. When we choose to keep knocking the Body apart because of our greed (for the next better job) and rebelliousness (because Americans must be independent, live on our own, and do our own thing) we cause pain to every part of the Body. The other issue in the social environment also related to greed or impatience, is our unwillingness to allow someone who is ill to take time to heal. In the countries where persons with mental illnesses simply take time out to get better, the long-term recovery rate is much higher.

Impact of medicines on human functioning. From a paper by Robert Whitaker, Carlene Byron adds this – "The medications used to treat mental illnesses alter the chemistry of the brain such that the brain cannot function normally without the medication OR WITH the medication after a fairly short period of time. This is why in our country, many people who are medically treated for mental illness get worse, not better. They are more likely to be disabled now that we have medical treatment than when we had none."

Now this might leave you disappointed and confused, and it might even seem contrary to what I have been saying in this book, but in reality it is not. Listen, the facts are these—we live in the society we were born into. Most of the readers of this book will be from the USA, and unless you plan on moving to Pakistan, we are trapped in the social dynamics that we have here in the USA. What this means is this, in a perfect world, which the USA is not, one would or should not ever need medication. When I counsel, my hope is that no one would ever have to go on medication. In most cases it is the means of last resort, but due to our present environment, taking a sabbatical for a few months to a year to get your head together and find solace with the Lord is impractical for most. Medication might be the only means we have. Again I say the only means we have when we are really emotionally disabled and so unstable that we can't function. In my case, when I fell into depression and anxiety, if I could have stopped working and moved to the mountains for a few months to heal, it might have worked, but reality dictated otherwise. I was dying, and daily functioning was coming to a radical end. I still believe medication (in my extreme case) saved my life, but—and there is that *but* again—there is a downside. When we begin taking medications, our minds adjust to that medication. In so doing our minds might not ever be able to live without them. Now many, many people have successfully been on medication and come off them, but again many, if not more people, never could get off them. Now I wanted to add this last note on medication to simply warn you of its dangers, and here is where I walk on a very thin, high wire rope. See, it's simply this. If we are in a bad way, we might have to take the medications to get out of it, but we also risk never being able to get off them. It is a gamble either way, and I cannot make that choice for you. It is simply the nature of the beast in Western society today and again, unless you have time to heal, which most of us don't. We might have no other option. With all that being said, I leave you again with this thought to ponder before you lash out at my stance on medication. You might be passionately against it, but don't be so quick to judge until you have a teen who is bent from society, weeping daily and unable to function. Seeing that child of yours in dire pain is a sure motivator to see them happy again. The question is, what would you do? Would you tell them to stick it out and possibly lose them or bite the bullet and try medications? What's sad is that we live in such a place where this has to be an issue. At the end of the day, the irony of it all smacks us across the face as the greatest, most prosperous nation in the world with the most stuff for personal pleasure, yet also the nation with the greatest rates of suicide, depression, and mental illness in general. I know there's a biblical lesson in there about contentment and our needs versus our wants. Problem is until that pendulum swings the other way, we are stuck in this mudhole called the United States of Mental Illness.

Next I would like to close out this chapter with ten myths about depression in particular that I found to be very true and worthy of repeating. Following is my list as I believe the Lord revealed them to me over the years.

Ten Myths about Depression

1. Depression will never go away.

    This is a lie as mine as well as millions of others has gone away.

2. Depression means I'm a weak person.

    This is a lie also as it didn't show how weak I was but how strong I could be in Christ.

3. Depression means I've failed as a Christian.

    Again, look at people who struggled with doubt, fear, and sadness in the Bible. Were they failures? I know that I am not as God is continuing to bless me. I didn't always see it this way, but I do now and you will too.

4. Depression for a Christian means never needing medication.

    Who says so? Not the Lord. I would not be here without it to help me to be able to listen to God again and do bigger things for Him. Again, not always the answer, but it can be one of them. Do not discount it as the Lord may be leading you to it.

    "Not by might, nor by power, but by my spirit, saith the LORD of hosts" (Zechariah 4:6). I have this scripture on my Christian counseling business cards. It is a constant reminder that my strength and wisdom can never heal or help me. It is only through the Lord's wisdom and direction that we can move on, and if medication be that wave to ride, well, I will ride that wave where it takes me as long as it takes me deeper into Christ.

5. Depression is best dealt with by secular professionals.

    The biggest lie, yet dependent on the type of depression, chemical or spiritual.

    Point here: *Ninety-five percent of depression and emotional problems are spiritual, so a Christian counselor or pastor who is well versed in depression and anxiety issues will be your best bet, but don't forget that you might need a medical doctor at times, and finding a Christian one can be hard if you do need medications. Ask your counselor for a recommendation, or if they have none, then ask the Lord to guide you to the right one.*

6. Depression means I have deep-seated mental issues.

   Then all those people in the Bible had them too, and it would also mean that I have deep-seated mental issues. Some people might debate that though (tongue in cheek).

7. Depression is always a result of sin.

   Sometimes, *but mostly not, in fact I believe it is one of God's greatest tools as He has used it over and over again throughout history. It works to get our undivided attention to Him, so why stop using something that works. Depression and anxiety are great attention getters.*

8. Depression is always a result of a traumatic life event.

   Can be sometimes—and this can determine where your depression is rooted in.

   Point 1: If it is based on a traumatic life event, then is it not abnormal as trauma always brings sadness? People get depressed when sad things happen, don't they? So why should you or I be any different?

   Point 2: We need to remember that life comes in seasons. *No one* is happy all the time. *"A time to weep, and a time to laugh; a time to mourn, and a time to dance"* (Ecclesiastes 3:4). This world is telling us that you should be happy all the time.

   Friend, *if you live to be happy all the time,* you are in for a fall. Life is very hard in case you haven't noticed.

9. My depression just affects me.

   Lie. *It actually affects everyone around you. Like when King Saul killed himself, others around him, also killed themselves*

   (1 Samuel 31:4–5). *Not that others will become depressed by your depression, but that their joy and peace will be hard to come by if they know the one they love so much is hurting. Be thankful for those who will share in your pain and suffering*

10. Depression is always a negative thing.

Here's the big surprise. Who says depression is bad? If that's true, then the Bible is a lie for the Bible says, "*All things work together for good.*" *Does that exclude depression then?*

See, when we look at spiritual and chemical / emotional depression for what it is, we see it not as an enemy, but as a blessing. It is like I have said over and over again. What if our emotional issues are simply a tool from the Lord? A tool to bring us to a higher place of having audience with Him. I don't know about you, but I hate going to the dentist. That drill is something I despise, but is it not needed to cut out the decay? I might hate it when I really should be thanking the dentist and the Lord for it. Also, to hate our dentist for using a drill is like hating the Lord for using depression and problems to heal our souls. As to medication, does not the dentist first give us a shot of Novocain before he begins drilling and sometimes some pain medication as we are healing afterward? I truly have learned to liken this analogy to the Lord's working with us through our depression and anxiety. And at the end of the day, be it after a major dental procedure or after the Lord has brought us through a great season of depression, we will certainly be able to smile again and in some cases smile bigger and better than ever before. "Let the drilling begin." And until you are able to say that to the Lord with full trust in Him, you will never be able to be all that He desires you to be.

But I'm Doing Everything Right. Why Now, Lord?

"And Joseph's Master took him, and put him into the prison, a place where the king's prisoner's were bound: and he was there in the prison."

—Genesis 39:20

Frustration. That's the only way I can describe emotional issues like depression and anxiety. Now, dear friend, this particular chapter might and might not apply to you and your situation, but it does apply to me and my story. If it is not your story, then please read it anyway as I know that you will pick up some important lessons that we all need to hear.

So my story is this, as I know it is for many. See, we think to ourselves—okay, I can understand emotional issues in the lives of drug-addicted movie stars and the unsaved that party their lives away. I can understand depression and anxiety for those of the world who do not know Christ and do not live according to His Word and way. But what I do not understand is why the righteous must also suffer. If you have ever thought those thoughts, then you know what I am talking about. You go to church, tithe your money; you are involved in ministries and sharing your faith with the lost. From mission trips to running your church's VBS program and Sunday school. All of these things you do and you do them for Christ with a heart for service. When others were going away on vacation, you were giving a week of your time to God by helping a tornado-stricken town get out from under the debris. Your whole life has been one of training your children and giving to the cause, and yet somehow the Lord knocks you off your feet and leaves you lying on the cold ground like a flopping fish that was just snagged. Maybe this isn't your story as depression comes from many places and for many reasons, but sometimes it comes, it seems, for no reason at all. These times of depression and anxiety are the hardest because they rock you to your core and leave you questioning if it is all even real. Working for Christ and yet getting nothing back from Him. Maybe He isn't even real and all of this was a waste of my years and money? In my life that's exactly what happened to me. I am not your typical case of anxiety and depression in regard to how it came upon me. There was no great trauma, no great loss, and no sudden life-shaking moment. In fact, all was going just fine for me. I was making the most money I ever made in the job of my dreams. I had a nice home, the wife and kids and the white picket fence. I was serving heavily in church and trying as hard as I could to never miss a service or church function. Of money I gave more than my tithe and made sure with every bonus and financial blessing that the Lord got His share. Family life was great, and all was just a dream as I remember saying so one day as I sat at a restaurant eating dinner with my family. I can remember these words like they were yesterday because I actually boasted about them to a mature Christian at church, who warned me to not say such a thing. What were the words that I said and secret thoughts that I had in my mind? "I have God all figured out, everything is perfect in life, and my system has God just where I want Him." Now I didn't say it just that way, but it is exactly what I was thinking. I was trusting in my system of bribing God to get what I wanted. I did my part, and as long as God did His, all would be peachy. I actually started to become quite a snobbish type of Christian, thinking that I had it right, and if you didn't do what I was doing, then you were wrong. If someone was struggling, I assumed it was due to sin. I began to judge everyone around me—be it their drinking and smoking or movie habits. See, I didn't watch R-rated movies or drink any alcohol, and I prided myself on my perfect Christian life. I only listened to Christian music, read Christian books, and made sure my firstborn son Jacob only played and watched Christian cartoons. I was the picture of extremism in all that I did, and my wife followed me down this path hook, line, and sinker. When a person came to me for counseling with depression issues and told me they had a chemical imbalance, I laughed it off and said, "Oh no, you just need to use the Scott system of salvation and path to happiness." I had no patience for people with such things, nor did I have patience with people on any level. When it came to my Christianity, I also became a snob and even began to think that my pastor and my church were the only ones who had it right. In time even the Christians that I hung out with were scrutinized, and if they didn't meet my level of doctrinal purity and maturity, then they were tossed to the side. I truly felt like a man safely in the hands of God due to my own labor and wisdom. I remember saying another dastardly thing one day by stating that God was like a genie in a bottle, and if you rubbed Him the right way, you got your wish. I sadly believed this to be true because God was allowing me to have all that I prayed for just to show me it was not what I really needed. When it came to praying, I also thought I was king as just about everything I prayed for came to be. People were actually becoming jealous of my audience with the Lord and believed I really did have some special in.

Now I say all this not to toot my own horn, but to explain the dangers of living for the wrong god. There is an old country Western song about looking for love in all the wrong places. Sometimes as Christians we are looking for happiness in all the wrong places. It is not found in faithful church attendance, in the giving of your money, in doing good deeds around the church, or in helping a poor animal out from the cold. No, it is only found in loving the Lord Jesus Christ with all of our heart, mind, and souls. If we do anything for any other reason, then because of that love for God and gratefulness of His wondrous gift of salvation, we live a life of disgrace and waste. Friend, there is no system to a good life, or a blessed life, but there is a way to the Father through Jesus Christ the Son. I'm not saying that I wasn't saved back then, but that I was misled through my motives. I had Christ as my Lord, but my life and my happiness was my only true desire. To suffer and feel pain was not part of my plan, and so when it came, it threw me for a loop. No, I was here for the joyride, not the spiritual ride of righteousness. This is why the Lord had to knock me off my high horse and rock my world. I tell you, I didn't see it coming because I thought I was doing it all right. How could or would God rock my world if I had the system all worked out, I thought. Well, He did, and I am glad He did. It wasn't fun, nor was it pleasant. In fact it was downright the worst thing I had ever experienced up to that time. Even in my worst, sinful, unsaved days of living deep in the world, I did not experience anything like I was about to enter into. Sometimes I like to say, "It was the worst of times; it was the best of times." To have it all in the palm of my hands and to systematically have it ripped from my hands was a painful lesson. See, the Lord had to tear me down right to my naked bones. Everything had to go— what I enjoyed, what I lived for, and what I trusted in. It all had to be taken away so there was no place to turn to but to God, and by turning, it meant turning to Him in a new and profound way. It was the place where I couldn't even breathe without His help. I couldn't eat without His help. I couldn't even think without His help. One might wonder how a loving God could put His child through such a thing. Well, it is because He is a loving God that He did and does what He must. In many ways He had to do this to me, or I would never see the deeper things of the Lord. I would never desire to enter into His throne room as a broken and desperate man. All pride, humility, and self-worth had to be ripped from my hands until I could lie there happy that I was broken and at peace with only being held by His hands.

The Fall

One day life was all that I had hoped it to be, and I was on my way up the ladder to success and greatness. Then in one fell swoop something began to change. It was as if the Lord pushed His celestial switch and nothing could be done to stop it until He deemed it time. I remember feeling just tired and just not right. I remember feeling weak and lethargic, but never anything to do with emotional thoughts or feelings. It really was all physical, which was why I took that route in trying to determine what was really wrong. I went from medical doctor to medical doctor. I would take test after test. My symptoms were cold sweats and numb, tingly arms. My skin always felt clammy and damp, but nothing really more than that. When I was through all the testing on the medical side, which all came back negative, I began to panic, but not in the traditional sense. I remember clearly the day I knew something was wrong. It was a trip I was preparing to go on with some men from church. It was to be a wilderness trek to the remote mountains where My father had a hunting cabin with a few four-wheel drive pickups and about four Christian men. It was a snowy January morning in 1996 and we were all ready to go. The night before I toyed with canceling as I was just not feeling right. I still could not put a finger on it other than something just wasn't right. I was sure I had the flu or some bug, and I was sure I had a temperature as I kept taking it every five minutes. I wanted to go on this trip so bad as it was an adventure I had dreamed about for years. Anyway that morning, as we met up, the snow was coming down, and I began to pray that the snow would fall harder so I would have an excuse to not go without looking like I was afraid. Well, the rest of the guys thought the weather was no big deal, so I was pressed to make a decision, as I didn't want anyone to know that I wasn't feeling right. I did what we often do when pride and fear gang up on us, and so I lied and made believe I was the mature one, and so I made the call that the roads were too dangerous. The trip was cancelled, and I drove home knowing that I was heading down a path I had never traveled. I unpacked my truck, undressed, and lay in bed as a tear rolled out and down from my left eye. I thought it strange that only one tear fell, and now looking back, maybe it was just the Lord telling me that it would be one of many. From that time on I knew I had to discover my sickness, which is what I called it. It would be a lady from church who has now passed on who kept telling me it was anxiety. I didn't want to hear her, nor did I want to believe her. Yet time brought me further down into confusion, and so I called her and asked her what anxiety was like. She told me about her symptoms and suggested I listen to an audio series on anxiety and how to fight it. That would be the worse thing I ever did—well, maybe not, as this road had to be traveled, but those tapes did unlock the door, which would not close again for many, many years. I remember lying in my bed on a sunny day and placing the headphones on my head as I played the first tape. Mind you this was not a Christian series, so Satan probably helped it along as it tore me apart. One by one the speaker would describe the symptoms of anxiety, and one by one they would appear in me. I don't know what exactly happened or if the Lord just let Satan have me, but by the time I was done with that series, I was crying hysterically into my hands thinking about what I had just discovered. At that moment full-blown anxiety hit me like being caught in a rainstorm with no umbrella and no place to hide. It would be a quick fall from mild anxiety to massive anxiety to paralyzing anxiety. Friends, it doesn't take long to figure out that living with full-blown anxiety is not how you want to spend the rest of your life. One year later, January of 1997, depression had set in and way surpassed my concern about my anxiety. Depression is like that, as it blocks out anything and everything but itself. I liken depression as a very selfish monster that only wants to feed itself. Depression is all about depression as it is all that you can think about. That empty, dark, and cold place where sorrow rules the roost. It would not be long that suicide became my only focus and thinking of ways to end my life my only passion. For me, I felt that nothing mattered, not family, not friends, and not even money. There was nothing that brought joy, and if there was anything joyful happening around me, it only made me sadder as it reminded me how I could not be a part of it and maybe never would. That is what's so bad about depression, the finality of it all. You just cannot seem to see past it or fathom that there can even be a past-it place. It is just here and now, and nothing else matters. Time and present darkness become locked in a wrestling match that no one can ever win. Of depression, it will drive you to places you never thought you would drive, thoughts you never thought you would consider, and sins you never thought you could conceive. All just to feel good again, and any cost seemed to be worth it.

Now many people at this time are probably saying 2 Timothy 1:7; that's all you need. Second Timothy 1:7 is it, grab hold of it and just move on. Well, I know that scripture well, but we need to know it better than well. It states that God has not given us the spirit of fear but of power, love, and a sound mind. This is true, but let's step back for a moment and ask ourselves this question: if God didn't give us the spirit of fear, it must mean that He knows we might have that spirit. And if we have the spirit of fear, we must ask ourselves, where does it come from? Friends, this is a very important factor, even more important today than it has ever been for the spirit of fear can come only from two places— our old sinful, doubtful nature and Satan Himself. I truly believe that the rise in anxiety today is not unlike the spirit of antichrist (1 John 4:3) that will permeate the world in the last days. Look around. It is not hard to see. This spirit of fear is like a plague rolling through our cities and towns. It is creeping into our homes and families. This spirit is not the Holy Spirit, but a spirit. It is a demonic delusion of despair and desperation. What's worse is that it is hard to avoid and much harder to shake once it clings to your mortal soul. It is like trying to avoid getting wet in a downpour. You can run as fast as you want through it, but unless you have an umbrella, you are getting wet. In our case the water is the spirit of fear and Christ is the umbrella. We must have it open and ready all the time and every day. If you think about it, once we do get wet in a rainstorm people can talk umbrella to you all day. They can yell, "Think dry thoughts!" but we all know that's not happening. Dear friend, that is why yelling 2 Timothy 1:7 at a depressed and anxiety-stricken person is just as foolish as yelling "Dry at a dripping wet person. Do you know what that wet person needs to do? They need to take some time, get out of the rain, change their clothes, and get dry with a towel. And even then they still might have a chill. The solution is to never get wet, which should be our ultimate goal, but if we do get wet due to the heavy rains falling lately, we need to take the next sometimes long steps of getting dry again. It is running to Scripture, to Christ, to a warm place of fellowship. It is hearing the good godly counsel of a soul who has been wet and now is dry. It is listening to the advice of those who know and who are equipped to give you the advice that is needed. So 2 Timothy 1:7 is a great scripture and one I personally hold dear, but we must also understand the flip side and this spirit of fear that is gripping our world. You are not alone and the Lord understands your pain. Build everything we are on Christ and a very deep understanding of His Word and we cannot go wrong.

Dear fellow sufferer, I added this chapter into the book to simply state the futility of life if life isn't built on Christ alone. Life is uncertain. One day you can be fine and within minutes it can all change. To the unsaved and even to the immature believer, this can be a curse or a blessing. Friends, we need to understand the unknowingness of life and be at peace with it if we are ever to succeed in it. Let me make it simple for you. Until you can get to the place where nothing matters except Christ, then you haven't gotten anywhere. Until you get to the place where knowing that your family, job, health, and all that you own can be removed or destroyed and it does not faze you, you haven't arrived at where the Lord wants you. Anxiety and depression seem to flow from many cracks in the mountainside, and one of the cracks that they flow from is that of life's fears. The fear of losing loved ones, position, and security. The fear of losing one's health and mobility. Even the fear of losing one's own mind. See, all of those things tie us up and bind us to them. Every day we live in fear of them possibly going away is another day we live in failure. We have to get to the point where none of those things matter anymore. You have heard me say throughout this book the term *glorious* depression, or the *wonderful* monster of depression. You might have thought me quite mad to say such a thing but not so when you find out what the Lord was doing all the while through our monsters of blessings, which are anxiety and depression. What was He doing but setting us free, free from the fear of anything and everything. Free to serve the Lord with no more concern of the what-ifs of living. Did we not wonder how the great saints of old and even our modern-day missionaries are able to do so much for the Lord and yet have so little. How do they do it? We wonder. How do they live knowing they have nothing to fall back on—no health insurance, no guarantee of their life not being snuffed out by some crazy killer in some terrorist-laden land? Today because of my training and boot camp from the Lord, I can now move forward without any fear of losing anything. At present time I have no health insurance as our little church can't afford to provide it for me and my wife. I fear it not, nor do I fear getting sick. I fear not losing my children, wife, or ministry because I have faced the worst fear, and that was losing my very soul. The Lord took me to a place that was so dark and so bad that nothing can ever be worse than it. There is nothing anyone can take from me that can be worse than being in that dark place. Certainly I'm not saying that I want those things to happen or that I wouldn't be devastated by them but that I don't fear them happening. The Lord is in control, and He proved that to me through this wonderful monster. He showed me His love, power, and majesty. I could not see it any other way, and though I would not wish to go through it again, I am certainly glad that I did. It is like writing a book, and though I can't place who said it yet, I know one famous author did when he penned these words, "I hate writing but love having written." Dear friend, it is a great soul pain to go through this chamber of horrors called depression and emotional bleeding, but I am sure glad that I did. I pray one day this will all make sense to you as it has to me. I know we wish that wisdom of God can be found some other way, but for many of the Lord's greatest laborers, it was the only way. If you are going through it today, I pray that you go through it quickly but not too quick. For those of you who have left it, I pray that you don't forget it and what good it has brought you, and if you cannot see the good, then you might have to enter in one more time. It will be over and it will be good. I have no other words for you but to hold on tight and never close your eyes. Sometimes by closing our eyes to avoid seeing the monsters, we also miss seeing the one who slays them. Take a peek during your dark days and see if you can see our Lord with His mighty sword cutting off that monster's head. Trust me, it's worth the peek.

We started this chapter with a scripture that might have seemed ill chosen, but I hope as we close out this chapter the choice might become perfect. In Genesis we read of Joseph, a great saint of the Old Testament. We read of his favor with the Lord and yet also the odd trials he was forced to face. In Genesis 39:20 we see him being punished, it seems, for just trying to always do the right thing. As a young man with his hormones ablaze, Satan presents him with a provocative temptress of a woman to release and fulfill his every desire, and yet he says no as he only wants to please the Lord. His whole life in fact was one focused on pleasing the Lord, but yet rewards don't seem to be what happens. Instead pain and suffering seem to be what follows every move toward doing the right thing. In verse 20 he is placed in prison only for resisting sin: "*And Joseph's master took him, and put him into the prison, a place where the king's prisoners were bound: and he was there in the prison.*"

Odd how the Lord would allow such a man of God to be placed in prison, thrown in a pit, sold for a slave. Yet in those dark places the Lord was preparing a man who would be placed in very high positions. Maybe all along what he thought was unfair treatment was actually just training. And to be honest, I don't believe Josephs thought it was unfair as he knew His Lord never made mistakes. Regardless, what's really important is what happens in verse 21 of Genesis 39: *"But the LORD was with Joseph, and showed him mercy, and gave him favour in the sight of the keeper of the prison."* The Lord showed him favor—yes, even favor in prison. The Lord is showing you favor also even in your prison of emotional pain and suffering. Be thankful for this favor and, before you know it, you will be serving the Lord in ways you could not imagine. Before provision must come faith in the Provider.

Simple Steps Before the Leap of Faith

"Wherefore the rather, brethren, give diligence to make your calling and election sure: for if ye do these things, ye shall never fall."

—2 Peter 1:10

Before we get into the simple steps to take to begin the healing process, I first want to speak a little bit about what you must do after you are healed. I know it seems backward to some degree, but I also believe in praising the Lord for healing before it has even come. That is why I want to begin this chapter with the things you must know and understand after you are healed. This way we are showing the Lord that we know we will be healed and believe it to such a degree that we want to begin preparing for it even before it happens. The Lord likes that kind of faith. So with all that said, let's look into the "after the fact" of post-healing living.

One of the things I enjoy doing is building and rebuilding things. I like rebuilding trucks and cars that are old and beaten up as well as building things out of wood. Take for example something that is rusted, worn out, and falling apart and making it like new. It is a very fulfilling feat. With anything that requires rebuilding, there must be a counting of the cost and the planning of the process. In restoring an old vehicle, you do not paint it before you make sure the engine is first running fine and the undercarriage is sound. This is also the same premise in rebuilding a life torn apart by depression and anxiety. Dear friends, the facts are that with radical depression and anxiety it can leave you with a mild to severe case of posttraumatic stress disorder commonly referred to as PTSD. In simple terms, it's the wounds that might have healed, but have not been forgotten. It is similar to a deep cut or incision from a surgery. The trauma to the body might have passed and now over, but the scar is forever there to remind you. Scars work two ways—one, as a reminder of something you never want to forget, or two, as a reminder of something you want to forget but can't. I don't think that scars forming on our bodies are by accident, but something that the Lord made part of our physiology. God seems to have this thing about reminders and remembering things. He is constantly reminding us that He never forgets His promises as well as reminding us that we should not forget His gifts and sacrifices as in the death of His only Son. Normally when we look at a scar, they are an ugly thing. The skin is hard and discolored and often grotesque compared to the rest of our body. They can be scary and might bring us anxiety about that event that caused it and it possibly happening again. They can also be a lifesaving reminder as in a scar from a burn or from a great fall where we played too close to an edge or fire. There they can remind us to never make that same mistake again. The saying "Once bitten, twice shy" is very true, and you and I would be wise to remember that. As we think about our emotional scars like those caused by depression and anxiety, we need to remember them in a positive way. Sure we can let them bring us down as we hash over and remember the pain and hurt, or we can look at them and say, "Look how far the Lord has taken me from there to now." In my second bout with depression and anxiety, I was plagued by a form of PTSD. I would begin to feel better and the healing began, but then something would remind me of how far I had fallen the year before, and this thought would trigger a relapse. The pain and darkness that I was in was so horrific to me that I just could not let it go. It truly frightened me to my core with a depth of fear that I have never known before. On a side note, sometimes I wonder if deep depression is a small picture of hell itself. A picture of a place where the separation from God is a worse pain than the lapping of the flames upon your skin. If hell is anything like depression, then I am truly glad the Lord let me taste its bitterness be it for a moment so I would never desire to go there ever again.

Okay, back to our discussion of scars and emotional pains. Let us make sure we look at everything in our lives the way the Lord does. As He states, for all things work together for good, then we must also look at all things as good for us even in the case of emotional pain. If they remind us of how far we have fallen and how great a rescue the Lord has accomplished in our lives from that pain, then it is a very good thing. As you look at your past pains or maybe current pains of today, let us remember that they will leave scars and wounds that might always be with us, but let us remember that a wound that has healed or will be healed is just that, *healed!* Forget what the past pain had caused upon you and look forward to what great healing the Lord has waiting for you. The greater the fall, the greater the Lord will have to work in your life and the greater the praise will be toward Him for such a great deliverance. Think of the stories that great scars can bring with them, and what great opportunities for sharing about God's working in your life. Just as a great hunter can boast of his many wounds and bear attacks, so can we boast of our many deep, dark cuts and how the master physician has sown them up so wonderfully. Do not be ashamed of your past or current wounds. Wear them proudly as pictures of training in the Lord's school of spiritual muscle building. I remember my first bout with depression and anxiety and how ashamed I was of it, especially being that I was a Christian. I would never want to talk about it, and certainly I never shared that I had to resort to medication to pull me back into the sun. Pride often accompanies great falls, and sin always comes with great pride. Remember, if sin be reigning in us, then the Lord cannot. Sin is the prayer blocker and let us not look at it any other way.

Now moving on, let's get to the point I wanted to make in this chapter. The point is about how we can and must move on toward healing. Dear friend, if you are in the midst of great emotional pain or just starting in its first phases of attack, let me give you some steps. These are steps that you can take to speed up the healing process. Steps that will hasten the learning process as this is all about learning. Did you just hear what I just stated? "This is a learning thing." It is not by chance that depression or anxiety has fallen upon you, but a place that the Lord has either allowed in your life or even purposely brought upon you. Yes, the Lord does bring pain and does allow hardship. He grows His greatest warriors in the soil of affliction. So for a first step let's look at it as entering college with a master's degree waiting on the other side. Look at it as many classes and credits that you must attain and of the many hours of papers, homework, and experiments you must deliver. There will be people that will test you and late-night hours that will try you. There will be setbacks and failing grades given. There will be long seasons of winter school years and some breaks of summer to regain your strength for the next semester. There will be times when the work load is so great that there will be no time for socialization, or time for relaxation. There will be those taking the test by your side that will seem to breeze through it while others might be far behind you. Each day, month, and maybe year should not be looked upon as a picture of a long battle, but as a reminder of how much closer you are today to graduation than you were the day before. During these classes we must also remember to keep our eyes on the prize. Just like that degree that we hang on our wall as proof that we have made it through and with nothing less than great wisdom to show for it. Let us also not forget Ecclesiastes 7:4: *"The heart of the wise is in the house of mourning; but the heart of fools is in the house of mirth."* Let us remind ourselves that great wisdom only comes through great suffering. Too much time spent under the blazing sun will only leave us blinded by it and unable to see what the Lord has been trying to show us. Let us also remind ourselves of what we do with a degree—to use it. If one graduates medical school, one does not take that degree and toss it in the closet and then work as a short order cook. No, you take that degree and hang it proudly and begin your task at healing other people with what the Lord has given you—that is, Wisdom. God's wisdom that is far greater than anything else we could ever attain. Proverbs 3:13–24 explains the benevolence of this wisdom from God through emotional pain.

Happy is the man that findeth wisdom, and the man that getteth understanding.

For the merchandise of it is better than the merchandise of silver, and the gain thereof than fine gold.

She is more precious than rubies: and all the things thou canst desire are not to be compared unto her.

Length of days is in her right hand; and in her left hand riches and honour.

Her ways are ways of pleasantness, and all her paths are peace.

She is a tree of life to them that lay hold upon her: and happy is every one that retaineth her.

The Lord by wisdom hath founded the earth; by understanding hath he established the heavens.

By his knowledge the depths are broken up, and the clouds drop down the dew.

My son, let not them depart from thine eyes: keep sound wisdom and discretion:

So shall they be life unto thy soul, and grace to thy neck.

Then shalt thou walk in thy way safely, and thy foot shall not stumble.

When thou liest down, thou shalt not be afraid: yea, thou shalt lie down, and thy sleep shall be sweet.

The Bible also speaks about running the race that is set before us, and also about how to run that race by keeping our eyes on Jesus Christ, the author and finisher of our faith. Through your season of healing, this concept of looking unto Jesus will become more critical than you can imagine and also at times very hard to do. Anyway, let's begin our lesson in baby steps before we get to any giant leaps of faith.

Survey the Terrain

Before I was a pastor, one of the many jobs that I had was operating a heavy earth-moving equipment and land grading. Grading a section of property with heavy earth-moving equipment is much harder than you think. One of the things you must do is climb down off your bulldozer and get on one knee. What this does is helps you spot the highs and lows of the terrain. The high sections need to be cut and the low sections need to be filled in order to make it all level. In most cases a surveyor comes in beforehand and marks the ground with grade stakes. They are small pieces of wood hammered into the ground and marked with a *C* for cut or an *F* for fill. There are many more marks, but these are the basic ones, and they instruct the dozer or grader operator in what to do. In our emotional struggles, we must do the same thing. We must be able to step away from ourselves to some degree and see what we will be facing. We must be able to look over the terrain of our lives and see what needs to be removed and what needs to be added. Sometimes like in the case of the surveyor we need an outside party to help us spot them. A person or persons who have godly wisdom and experience to see what maybe we cannot. Being human, our problem is that we are not good at spotting faults and weaknesses in our lives. Sometimes a trusted brother or sister in Christ can see it much better. In a perfect world I would suggest a Bible-based Christian counselor, yet even then remember that it is the Holy Spirit that ultimately will bring us to see what we need to see. People can tell us about our faults all day, but until the Lord convicts us of it, we will never change. So again, survey your life. Are there people who need to go that are a deterrent to your mental well-being? Are there life habits that might appear okay to us but to the Lord they are destructive? I see this often in people I am counseling, and it is by far one of the least addressed issues. That is of the company we keep and where that company brings us spiritually. For example, I have counseled many people who are in great turmoil and yet they refuse to give up their old lifestyle and friends. Dear friends, please listen to me. You cannot serve Christ and find His healing if you're still hanging out at bars and nightclubs with people who know nothing of Christ. We can't be sleeping with a person and having sexual relations out of marriage and expect the Lord to change anything. What we do by refusing to let go of these things is to say to the Lord that we make the rules and we decide what needs to go and what needs to stay. So many people complain to me about God's failing them while in reality they are failing God. All the ways of the world must be left behind, and if you choose to not release them, then you are choosing to never be healed. Sin must go if prayers are to be answered. Righteousness must be desired more than pleasure if deliverance is to be had. If we call ourselves followers of Christ and yet live and look like the world, then how can we be truly His children? So many of the people that I deal with will tell me about their pain, sorrow, and years of depression and crippling anxiety, but yet post things on their social media pages that are an abomination to the God they say they follow. So many people are in so much pain, yet they refuse to hear anything about the realities of God in their life and how He must be preeminent in all of whom and what we are. In many cases the problem is one of simple self-love above God love. We simply love our sex, drinking, drugging, and party lifestyle more than anything else. Dear friend, remember that at the end of the day, "everything" is about "one" thing, and that is getting us to a place of flat-out worship, service, and love for the Lord Jesus Christ. It is about nothing else but that, and until we see that, we will see no healing, growth, or change. Many times our lack of healing is simply due to our lack of desire for Christ. Sure we want Him, but only as a means to get what we want. If Christ can help me fine, but just as we hire a mechanic to repair our car, once that car is running again, we have no need for that mechanic. With God He doesn't want to be used but instead to be fallen in love with, and if you don't really want Him as Lord in and over your life, you are really telling Him that you only want to use Him. Your depression and your anxiety or whatever trial that befalls you only bring you to Christ and make you more like Christ. Getting back to surveying your life, do it quickly while taking notes and write it down if you must. Take a spiritual inventory of your past, present, and where you would like to see yourself in the future. Then place that list next to God's standards, goals, and desires and see how they compare. If they are miles apart, then your healing is a long way off. Remember our goal is not to be better people or a happier people, but better and more fruitful Christians. After we have removed the issues of concern in our lives, then we must begin to survey to see the lows that need to be filled in. Do we have enough prayer, praise, Bible study, and Christian fellowship in our lives? Are we motivated by the right reasons in even attending Bible studies and church services? Are we trying to trick God into healing us by showing up at every church event when we really would rather be somewhere else? Do we read daily devotions to get better or to get closer to Christ? It is my goal in this devotional book to not just show you where healing is found but to show you where Christ is found and why Christ is everything. The Lord wants servants, not those who constantly need to be served. If you go to church to find out what they can do for you and never what you can do for Christ, then you come selfishly. Sure we might be at a place where we can only receive and be ministered to, but that is never where the Lord wants us forever. Sooner or later He wants us giving back and bringing others to Christ. Being a receiver only was never meant to be a lifestyle but simply a ladder to greater ministries in Christ. How is your financial giving to your local church? Are you simply looking at your offerings as payment for services rendered or services promised? Motivation, motivation, motivation—they are the trinity of successful living in Christ. Have your motivation off in any part and that part has become corrupted.

Begin a Daily Regimen of Praise

Praise is something that took me a long time to understand and sadly I feel it is one that many if not most Christians will never get. Now that might seem like a bold statement as you see so many Christians with arms raised high in praise every Sunday morning. But that's not the praise I am talking about and sadly the praise that most think God is looking for. Now before I go off too much on the phony circus show that has become the modern church service of today and the pastors that have become nothing more than circus ringleaders, let me instead focus on what true worship of Christ really is. Now don't get me wrong, I love a good worship service and good worship music, be it contemporary or traditional hymns. They are all great and wonderful in their proper order and place. No the praise that the Lord is waiting for is something more, something deeper something far beyond our once a week observance as we coldly mouth some words. No it is the ability and sincerity of truly thanking the Lord for your current situation. Not just a flippant mention of thanksgiving like we do before we eat dinner but a real actual cry of praise. Praise to the God of all creation who we believe cannot do anything but good things. Praise to our Lord in which we trust with our very lives to lead us where we need to be. Dear friend, this type of praise is what we need to invoke even at the darkest places of depression and anxiety. To honestly say to our Lord that we are grateful for this place of pain that He is deemed best for us to partake of. To say it and mean it and know that even in this present pain our Lord reins supreme. That He is large and in charge and we are happy that He is. This has truly been the hardest place for me personally to come to but one that once I did arrive in did change everything. I must admit that this nugget of wisdom came from a lady that I was counseling for years who had the worst depression and anxiety I have ever seen. She told me that her greatest triumphs always came after true praise for her pain. And might I add that today she is healed and living a victorious life in Christ. The power of praise, dear friend, is the most powerful tool in our belt. Not just once a day either, but every time the monster of gloom and pain comes upon us. It should be like a reflex of our soul. A reflex that in time would become as natural to praise God in trials of pain as it is to smile when a large check comes in the mail. Praise begins with that very simple act of truly trusting our Lord. What it says is simply this, that we are so confident and sure of God's love for us that if He deems it good for our soul to suffer for a season, we would truly be thankful for it. Not my will but Your will be done, dear Father and Lord of all creation. Learn this, friend, and watch what happens.

A Preemptive Strike—See Things As They Really Are

As we are going through baby steps to emotional health, please note that I am starting with the bare minimum here. Before we start counseling and possibly medications, I want to go after the simple things first. Being that I have no idea of what level your emotional pain is, I have to start with basic life anxieties and depression and move on from there. Let's face it. Life simply on its own merits always has moments where anxiety and seasons of melancholy will pop up. If you never have those down seasons, then something is wrong, as somber moments in life sometimes offer us the most growth potential in life. As you have heard me say before through this book/devotional/project, going for the simplest things first has often proven in my life to be the most successful, so it is then worth a try. If you are dealing with depression and or anxiety, don't just jump into psychiatric care and or medication unless your individual case warrants it. Jumping too fast and too deep into treatments that are far too heavy is as bad as taking chemotherapy for a sunburn. What I have found is that looking at things in their proper perspective often puts things in a more realistic bubble. Things like money issues, health issues, romantic issues, and family issues. Each one of them can cause depression or anxiety, but to what degree they are causing our depression and anxiety is really up to us. One successful way at looking at issues that you feel are causing you emotional pain is to ask this question of them. "Where would they really leave you?" Take for example the economy, many people are having great anxiety about such things, and if left unchecked, they can lead us to unwarranted anxiety. "Will I end up living in the streets, begging for bread, alone and out in the rain?" Sometimes our minds actually bring us to that place, but what is the reality of that happening? Dear friends, a lot of our anxieties can be taken away with one broad stroke of a brush when we see them next to the Word of God. The Bible says that the Lord will never leave us or forsake us. It promises that we will never be begging for bread, or left for dead. Either that is true or it is not. Our daily bread is a promise from the Lord, and what we need to only understand is this. What we need versus what we want—this might be the real cause of our fears. True, without money I might lose the ability to buy a new cell phone, new TV, new home, and maybe I might have to drive an old clunker of a car, but the Lord never promised us those things anyway as they are not *needs* but simply desires. At the end of the day, as long as I have Christ as Lord, then there is nothing that my problems and current difficulties can do to me that Christ cannot overcome. It really comes down to being able to accept the Lord's will for your life above your own will. See, we want the new car, the new large-screen TV, but we really don't need them, and what it really becomes is a matter of pride. What will my friends and family say if I am poor? This is where the prosperity gospel has really done great harm, by which it has actually added more anxieties to life than removed them. We simply are told that we should be wealthy in Christ to be happy in Christ. In time we believe that, and when we see things turning down a bit, we then begin to panic. What of all the Christians in remote or third-world countries, are they any less loved or blessed by Christ? We better be careful with that answer as most of those poorer nations have much more peace in Christ than we do. The less you have, the less you fear losing it. Nothing to lose equals nothing to fear. This is really the mindset we should all have. Prosperity has actually cursed us into a nation of anxiety by simply giving us more things to fear losing. I often think of people in the forties during WW2 living in the USA and other parts of the world as well. They didn't have much, they lost a lot, and though they might not have been happy, they surely were not clinically depressed or battling with anxiety. Why is that? Why are we suffering today with record amounts of anxiety and depression here in the USA? Could it be because we don't know how to have little? Why is it that the generation today, with the most possessions that any other people have ever had since the beginning of time, is also the most depressed and fearful? I truly believe that Satan has masterfully made us a fearful, untrusting, ungodly people just by letting us have all of our desires. It is like letting a child live in a candy store. At first he is thrilled at the idea until later he is sick because of that same candy.

Now let's get back to seeing things as they are. Let's also try this approach in other areas. Say you have had a bad loss in the area of romance. You are alone and your heart is broken. You can only see yourself as dying broken and in a dark room with no one to love you or care for you. Will that really happen, and what is the worst-case scenario? Is not the Lord able to bring new loves into your life, to bring joy even when you are alone? Are all single people destined to live in depression and sadness? If that be the case, then Paul should have been on antidepressants since he had no wife, no money, and no health for the most part and left alone in a prison cell. How was he able to keep on serving and believing? Was it not because he trusted only in Christ and Christ was all he really needed? Yet Paul was fed, and clothed, and comforted, maybe not to our standards of today but according to God's standards.

On a side note about depression and today's generation, I have often thought about this. I believe that this generation of people in their forties to fifties are going to end up being the most depressed generation in their seventies and eighties that have ever lived. I thought about this one day as I was visiting a nursing home for a person from my church. I saw all the wonderful gray-haired people there all dealing with life's downturn and accepting the fact that they would have to be satisfied with a shuffle board and with feeding the birds. The music in the hallways played was that of the big-band era. Then all of a sudden I had a vision of my generation and what a nursing home would look like twenty years from now. Would we have heavy metal playing over the PA? Would we be sitting in wheelchairs with all of our wrinkled tattoos and body piercings? Would we be so quick to accept the quiet life when for all of our lives it was drunken parties, crazy sex, and busy cell phone affairs. Extreme living was all that we knew and quiet time of contemplation was something that we feared more than death itself. Would the words from a once-famous rock band from the sixties that said "I hope I die before I get old" be our mantra? I truly see a future generation where getting old and slowing down from the dancing and party life might just kill us. I see suicide escalating to new heights, and depression and people on medication reaching epidemic levels. Simply put, because of how we were raised today and how we process living with out God and the afterlife, we will end up being the generation that didn't know how to get old. Proverbs 17:22 seems to jump out as a scripture that will haunt our future geriatric generations: "*A merry heart doeth good like a medicine: but a broken spirit drieth the bones.*" If our spirits be broken today, how can we rejoice in our future when we believe that life without passionate playing isn't living at all? Just a simple thought to ponder and I felt worth adding to this work of the mind.

Next let us deal with the worst of the worst two issues that can cause great depression and anxiety: the loss of a loved one and or the loss of your own personal health. If we have cancer and or a loved one dies from cancer, what then? Does God stop being God? Does He stop being able to comfort, protect, and guide us? These fears are really the problem more than the problem themselves. Fear of getting cancer can do more damage than having it. Dear friend, if we die from cancer, where do we go in Christ? We are forever with Him and no longer in pain. If we lose a loved one to cancer, though it might tear us apart, cannot the Lord rebuild us again? If we think not, then we don't know our Lord, and if that be the case, you are simply living in fear because you don't believe that God's Word is true. Please understand me. I am not downplaying the horrific loss of a loved one to cancer, rape, and accident. Losing a child is even more painful, and I pray I never have to face that loss, but if I did, what would I do with Christ? I once heard a pastor say and say it so well that we should never get to the place with God where we tell Him, "Lord, I love you and will serve you with all my heart, but if you take my wife or child, then I am through with you." Dear friend, is that not what we are saying or thinking when anxiety comes upon us by these thoughts and fears? We must be able to get to the place where our love and trust in Christ is so great that we can boldly say, "The Lord gave and the Lord takes away, blessed be the Name of the Lord." "Lord, I love You and trust You, and if You must take my dearest away from me to make me into who you desire, then so be it." If you can't get to that place, then fear will fill that place. Yet what's so wonderful about being in that place is that once there, fear and anxiety has no place to live. Like a parasite needs a host victim to live off, so does fear and anxiety. Take away its food and you starve it to death. What's even more amazing is that sometimes the Lord uses depression and anxiety themselves to bring us to that place, and once there, we never have to go back there again.

Even more so, let's say the worst happens and all of your worst nightmares come true, which most of the time this is not the case, but anyway, what would you do? Maybe you might need counseling. Maybe you might need medication. Maybe you might have some tough times of working past these pains, but if the Lord be with you, then you are never truly alone. Nothing is truly over in your life. Nothing is done and complete until the Lord says so. Early on in his life and ministry, Oswald Chambers died, leaving his young wife behind. Instead of becoming a recluse and hiding from society, she decided to gather all of her husband's sermons and notes and put them into books and devotionals. Maybe without him dying we would never have had his great works to give us comfort today. Now I would like to clarify something here. If you have not Christ, you just may have to face a life of depression and ruin. But if you do, well, it's never over. It's never done, and we are never defeated and forgotten. Dear friend and fellow sufferer, if Christ be the Captain of our ship, shall we not make it to the port He has prepared for us?

Begin and End Right

Each day we arise is a new day to serve and also to learn. Remember the school of training you are in and the goal of righteousness you aim to reach. To start each day in Christ is to start each day in prayer, scriptures, and devotional time. Interesting, I began my greatest morning and evening studies after I went through my greatest bout with emotional pain. I decided, or should I say, the Lord decided, that each day should be started and completed with connection to our King. Sad that we have no trouble checking our e-mails, the newspaper, TV news, and all the social media in the morning to find out what's happening in the world, but we have no time to find out what God has happening in ours. My wife and

I made it a commitment to start each day and end each day with at least something of God. For the most part our recipe is this, prayer and praise for the day ahead. Then we read a daily devotional and then a section of scriptures out of a daily Bible system. At night we do the same. We praise Him for everyone coming home safely and read one or two devotionals depending on our moods. Do we ever miss a day or night reading, yes and sadly so, because we feel other things must be done, but for the most part we have been pretty faithful. Now, dear friend, I know what some of you might be thinking, "What about the days that I am paralyzed with anxiety and or depression, do you expect me to even attempt such a thing?" My answer to that is no, but the Lord's answer certainly does. Yes, it's hard, darn hard, and I would in my dark days barely have the strength to get out of bed, let alone pray and praise the Lord, but nonetheless it was what He demanded, and so I did it. Through the anger, pain, and panic I tried as hard as I could to praise Him. Through the times when I was so sick from panic that I was throwing up, nauseous, and barely eating enough to stay alive, I still would pace around outside sometimes in the dark praying and praising Him. Sure I was also begging for healing and wisdom as the tears rolled down my face, but I knew praise was key, if I was ever going to prove my blind trust in the Lord. Another thing that I would recommend is going to bed with some type of system playing scriptures. I had this neat DVD that would show the Bible pages and you also heard a voice reading them. When I didn't have the strength or desire to read, I would let that system or even a close friend read me to sleep. Yeah, it does get that bad sometimes that you actually need that, but maybe that's what the Lord wanted all along, to have audience with us when normally He would only get our leftover scraps of time. Maybe if we go to our knees daily in prayer, the Lord doesn't have to bring us there through pain. And by the way, going down on your knees is not a silly notion but a mandatory one. Those who kneel before the Lord can stand before kings and princes.

Practical Tips

As we have spoken about in other parts of this book, diet and exercise can be of great importance. Not as much as some people would lead you to believe, but enough to help you a bit. Caffeine can be a good friend or a nasty enemy. Sugar, vitamins, herbal supplements, and even acupuncture can help also. I personally make sure my vitamin D is up to par as per a blood test. During the winter and for you who live in a sunless region, keeping this up can make a difference in your moods. Many don't know this, but some sugar substitutes are actually known to cause depression, as well as some prescriptions and over-the-counter cough medicine. It is always good to read the possible side effects to all over-the-counter and prescription medications alike. Also you might want to check your testosterone levels if you are male as recent studies have shown extreme low levels in this area play a very big part in depression and all of its side effects. A simple blood or urine test could find this out and have you on the road to recovery. Just ask your doctors. Even some antidepressants can cause depression and suicidal thoughts, but as I have discussed earlier, that is only in very high doses and unique to each person's physiology. Not to deviate off topic here, but in regard to medications, always remember that there is no magic medication or better medication. Any good psychiatrist will tell you that it's not so much the medication but which one works on you. One medication that works wonders with your body's makeup might do absolutely nothing for me and in fact make me feel worse. That is the downside to medication in that it's a crapshoot in finding the right one. Sometimes you get it on the first try, and in other cases it can takes years, but that's not the norm, so fear not. Okay enough about medication and back to the real healer, which is Christ, who by the way can help you get the right one on the first try, and that is one thing the unsaved world does not have.

Moving on with practical tips, here is another. Sleeping and how much of it you are getting. This is very hard, dear friend, and it will take all of your will in this area, but sleeping issues are a big part of emotional problems sometimes. Sleep too much and your anxiety is going to trigger itself much quicker. Yet if you are suffering with depression, sleep is all that you want to do. Sleeping late and or all day are very bad habits that are very hard to break. If you do anything, please stay out of bed as much as possible and stay active. There is very little healing that goes on under the covers. Once your normal hours of sleep needs are met, sleeping more hours only does harm. For one, getting up at 11:00 a.m. or later leaves you always with a feeling of depression as the day is and has slipped past you. I believe in many ways sleeping can actually turn to sin if we are using it as a drug to hide under as well as time that is stolen from God for self. In many cases running home to bed becomes like an alcoholic running home for a drink. The Lord will not have it and will make sure you don't heal through it. Now getting away to some quiet place is another story. I highly recommend getting outside, by the ocean, mountains, or anywhere the Lord's creation is seen. Getting away from the noise and hustle and bustle of life is important also, but that does not mean sleep. It will be a battle, and it will help to have a loved one who has a strong enough will to sternly get you out of bed and make you get up and ready for life. Life happens out there, friend, and getting up and ready to face it might be a great struggle for us, but it is one we must reach for.

Also in our morning routines, let's not forget to shower and get dressed. You men out there, let's make sure we shave and let's put on some *going-out* clothes, meaning no wearing of pajamas or sweats all day long. Sure it sounds like it wouldn't matter, but believe me, it does. It is a signal to our mind and confidence that the day has begun, and we must face it. Another great but simple tip is walking, and walking in Christ, if I might add. Exercise is very to somewhat important, but at least try walking if you just can't bring yourself to a cardiovascular level. Listening to praise and worship music is another simple but amazingly powerful tool. Get those earbuds in and get out. For the weather, well, the sun is our friend. Winter and rainy seasons are not our friend, and these can be the worst seasons for us. The sun is an amazing wonder of the Lord as it brings life to the animal and plant kingdom. It also brings life to us. If you can afford it, try a tanning salon for some rays, but nothing beats the real thing. For the temperature, well, that's another area of interest. Some people do better in the heat, some in the cold. As a general rule, cooler is better for anxiety and heat for depression.

Another area where depression and anxiety differ is in the area of socialization. Crowds are not a friend to anxiety, and being alone is not a friend to depression. If you are struggling with depression, please *do not* stay away from church and fellowship. If I hear another person telling me that *as soon as they feel better they will be back to church*, I think I will burst. Hibernating is not good, and it is also not scriptural. We are not to forsake the assembling of ourselves together. We need to worship and share time with other believers. Even a simple night out having some coffee or tea with a friend (decaf). Jesus told us that the church is a place where we share each others joys and sorrows. We can't do that watching some mega church evangelist on TV when we should be supporting and attending our local assembly. People who think that watching Pastor so and so on TV is their church service are not well versed in Bible theology. A church worship service is just that, a worship service with other likeminded believers.

These are all just simple steps we can take, yet most radical leaps of faith to healing take much longer. Yet let us not forsake these little things that will certainly help us with the bigger ones. Baby steps are just that. They are tipping that toe in the water after you have been sitting on the beach for too long. Jumping right in might work for some, but our type of pain and trauma normally takes a very gentle and careful approach. Make and take your steps wisely and as our starting scripture says *by application*. We have a mission and a calling, and if we are to find out what the Lord has for us to do, we then must use great diligence in choosing the path to healing that He has prepared for us. And if we find the path He has chosen and we don't falter from that path, we will never fall.

> *Wherefore the rather, brethren, give diligence to make your calling and election sure: for if ye do these things, ye shall never fall. (2 Peter 1:10)*

Starting to Crawl

So we have gone over all the little things that we can do, all the foundational building blocks on which we can begin the healing process. We have spoken about the dangers, the warnings, and the tools that the Lord has laid at our feet if we but use them. We have discussed what anxiety and depression are and why it might be entering your life. We have discussed the obstacles and ignorant opinions that might be spoken against and about you. Of medication and the other many ways the Lord might use we have spoken about them too. We have looked at biblical examples and how the Lord has raised up the greatest of people by using His greatest tools, which are depression and fear. Yet with all of that that we have spoken about, we still haven't moved an inch forward unless we move an inch forward. Dear friend, this is where the rubber meets the road, where we separate the men from the boys, if you will. It is here at the desire to move forward that all this must take place. Today is the day that you must make that first step. No one can or should make it for you, and just as any type of healing begins with desire to be healed, so it is with you and me today. This is critical. This is the moment. This is where all the angels in heaven bend their eyes and ears to watch and listen for what a child of God will do when faced with the greatest test of their lives. And as the angels in heaven rejoice over one sinner that repents, so will they rejoice with you when they see that first step of obedience. Now I can't prove that second part scripturally, but I know one thing, and that is that the Lord will surely rejoice when He sees you get up and put those two feet on the ground. What do I mean by all this, and what am I trying to say? I am trying to say this. You must get up and decide to fight. Lying in bed must come to an end. Reading this book and the many other self-help books that I am sure friends have given you must be put down eventually. There comes a time when we simply need to face the music, to say to ourselves that it's time to start fighting. I was there, and that moment was a turning point. I had people to serve, souls to lead to Christ, and a family that needed me. Hiding in bed needed to be a thing of the past and leaning on Christ must begin. No more complaining (which is sin), no more trying to get other people to help you or support you. There can be no more excuses and no more date setting, which means no more saying that next Tuesday you will begin or after I sleep a little more. No it must be now, it must be real, and you must step out with that first foot placed onto the water. Will it be easy? No way as I will be the first to say it was the hardest thing I have ever done, but nonetheless it must be. I remember the day when I dragged myself out of bed and stood looking in the mirror. I was weak, afraid, and in the middle of a massive panic attack. Sweat was dripping off me like a shower, and the clock was ticking. There was no reprieve either as the Lord really wanted to test my faith muscle to see if it was really faith holding me there. The training wheels were taken off, the cast was removed, and the bandages unwrapped. It was now or never, and I chose now as I couldn't face the other any longer. See, friend, it truly must get worse before it gets better. It needs to be a worse place to be in that bed than out of it. I needed to get to the place where I couldn't stand it or myself anymore. Living this way was not living, and if there was such a thing as hell on earth, it was this pain. I believe the Lord really brought me to that place where the pain was so bad that getting back into life was less of a pain. So I got myself dressed and I marched over to the duties I was given. By the way, this all happened on a Sunday morning before I was to preach. It was about fifteen minutes before I was getting ready to preach to be exact. It was stand up and walk on the water or turn in my papers and decide to give up on everything that I so strongly believed in or at least I thought I did.

Dear friend, the Lord did carry me that day, but He didn't lend me a finger until I stepped out on the water and placed my full weight on His unseen truth. Now I would love to tell you that from that day I was healed and I happily skipped along back into life. No, that didn't happen, but what did was my will to follow, believe, and get real or give up became alive. In time I did begin to heal, and yes, there were some setbacks, and yes, there were more days like that, ones where I had to fight for every inch. Was it worth it? Is it worth it for you? Well, you know what I am going to say. I am healed. I am better and stronger than I ever could have imagined. I am a new man in Christ, and as I have often said, I feel like I was born again, again. Would I want to go back to those days? Surely not, but if the Lord deem it, then who am I to say no. It does get better, and the Lord is real. He will heal, and He will bring you to greater heights of service. So take that deep breath and say, "Lord, today I must begin to follow you, maybe for the first time in my life, but it must happen, and today is that day. In thee I place my trust." In Jesus's name, amen.

Light, Glorious Light of Victory

"He will swallow up death in victory; and the Lord GOD
will wipe away tears from off all faces; and the rebuke of His
people shall He take away from off all the earth: for the LORD
hath spoken it.
And it shall be said in that day, Lo, this is our God; we have
waited for Him, and He will save us: this is the LORD; we
have waited for Him, we will be glad and rejoice in His
salvation."

—Isaiah 25:8–9

"We are almost there." Remember those words when you were a child riding in your parent's car? "Are we there yet?" So often I remember those words, and so often am I reminded of those words through my own children. The excitement of getting to a desired destination is one that is almost unmatched. For those of us who were in or are in the grips of depression and anxiety, the question of its departure is one we ponder often. If I had a dollar for how many times I asked the Lord *how much longer* I would have some dollars to spend. Too often that dream seemed to be a vanishing one, and the longer it tarried, the more depressed I became. This is normal and to be expected, but it is not truth. The truth is that healing will come, joy will be in the morning, and there will be an end to this suffering. In this chapter I want to focus on that day and why it's a certainty to happen. Friend, if there be no hope of that day, then we are a hopeless people serving a hopeless God. As the apostles said, "*If there is no resurrection then we are most miserable and we might as well just eat, drink, and party our life away.*" If that were true, friend, then I would not be wasting your time with this book. If Christ be not real, then I would have taken my life long ago or have gone off into wretched sin and wickedness. I am not a fool, and if my Lord be a lie, then I would certainly know it. I would never have felt His hand of deliverance or His gentle guiding in love and compassion. But He is real and I have felt it. I have been delivered, and I have seen the greater purpose in this all. Victory is coming, dear friend, so please lose not heart. The scriptures are manifold in this area, and I would like to share a few with you.

> *For whatsoever is born of God overcometh the world: and this is the victory that overcometh the world, even our faith. Who is he that overcometh the world, but he that believeth that Jesus is the Son of God? (I John 5:4–5)*

In Christ we can do all things, overcome all things, and accomplish all things according to His will.

> *I have written unto you, fathers, because ye have known him that is from the beginning. I have written unto you, young men, because ye are strong, and the word of God abideth in you, and ye have overcome the wicked one. (1 John 2:14)*

If we be not overcomers, then what is the use, but we are, and in Christ we are more than that. Also notice that in 1 John 2:14, John points out what constitutes one who is strong and an overcomer. It is one who knows the Word of God, and even more the Word of God lives in you and through you by how you walk and live this life. It is very important that the Word of God is our standard and plumb line by which all we do is weighed. It is the Word of God where power, wisdom, and guidance are found. Without the Word of God we are no greater than the world. We are lost, alone, and defeated. You could take medication for twenty years, see the best counselors and therapists, but if Christ's Word doesn't flow through your vein, you are weak and undone. The Word is everything. Make no mistakes about it. It is our compass, our guide, our life source, and our connection to our King.

> *But thanks be to God, which giveth us the victory through our*
> *Lord Jesus Christ. (1 Corinthians 15:57)*

I like it that it is Christ that gives us the victory because if it was up to me, I wouldn't have made it. But Christ does give us the victory, and it is just up to us to believe that it is true. It is up to us to believe that it is coming and to believe that He also desires for us to have it. Dear friend, it is of no worth to the Lord if we go down in a ball of fire. It is of no use to the Lord if our testimony crumbles and we take our life. No, it is of great value to the Lord if we are victorious so the unsaved world can see it and know that it was of something much greater than ourselves. Sometimes I think that's why the Lord uses such weak vessels like me and you because when we do *light up* again for Him, the world must conclude it was something greater than ourselves because they knew us to be but mice of fear and small stature. God will deliver you because you're the greatest testimony to His redeeming work.

> *Ye are of God, little children, and have overcome them: because*
> *greater is he that is in you, than he that is in the world. (1*
> *John 4:4)*

Notice in this scripture where the power comes from to be an overcomer? It only comes because Christ dwells in us. Being religious, nice, and giving to the poor might make you feel good about yourself, but if Christ doesn't dwell in you by faith alone, then you are alone. A simple analogy would be this. You are an army tank, you are painted military green, you have massive guns mounted all over you, yet you have no engine. Dear friend, we can look as religious and holy as we want, but if Christ be not driving us, we are dead in the water—immobile, weak, useless, and powerless to fight the battle that the world lays in wait for us. Christ must be the captain of your vessel, the engine of your soul, the water that you drink, and the food that you eat. No, not by religious observance, or denominational affiliation, but by being reborn and made new through repentance and acceptance of Christ as total Lord of your life. Not by good deeds that you have done, but by what Christ has done on the cross for you. Trust in anything else and you are trusting in self and others. If that be the case, then you can't be trusting in the Lord 100 percent.

A Psalm. O sing unto the LORD a new song; for he hath done marvellous things: his right hand, and his holy arm, hath gotten him the victory. (Psalm 98:1)

One of the characteristics of one who is an overcomer in Christ is the attitude of praise. We must not be complainers or whiners, but only those who can sing unto the Lord during the day no matter what we face during the night. It is to understand that the victory we are shouting about is that of forgiveness for our sins, salvation from judgment, and a place in heaven and deliverance from hell. That is why we praise His name and for those reasons first and foremost. If we only praise Him for financial blessings, and good fortune, then we miss the point of the cross. We are a redeemed people, and if you are not first grateful for that and if needs be only for that, then you will never be a grateful person for anything. Life is hard, troubles come, sickness may trip us up, but we must still rejoice because we are victorious over death and the grave. Today so many are praising the Lord for a good life here and now, which is fine, but Christ didn't die for a good life here but for a place reserved for you and me in heaven. A place paid for with Christ's own blood as a ransom for our sins. Our sins are forgiven, and if you don't think that's a big deal, then you don't even know why you came to Christ. Please, dear friend, don't come to Christ to end your depression and anxiety, but come to Him because He is Lord of all and you know that you can't approach this Lord of all unless you be made righteous. Millions of preachers and pastors today are telling people to come to Christ for a good life when He never promised a good life but a life of victory over sin. Come first through that door, and yes, yes, He can heal your depression and anxiety, but only if we can be grateful first for our forgiveness of sin. I know it is not what you've been hearing out of most of the pulpits lately, but that's the truth and the sooner you understand that truth, the sooner you will be delivered. First Timothy 1:15 says this clear as day, and if your pastor is not preaching this, then ask him why, *"This is a faithful saying, and worthy of all acceptation, that Christ Jesus came into the world to save sinners; of whom I am chief."*

He came and died and rose again to save sinners from what? He came to save sinners from the fires of judgment and hell. Be grateful for this, dear friend, and the Lord will find pleasure in you because of it. Imagine if you could for a moment give a very large gift to your child, say you bought them a new car for graduating college, and yet they send you a thank-you card for buying them ice cream when they were five years old. We can see then from that example how the Lord is feeling. He gave His own Son for our sins, yet we thank Him for having a nice day at the beach. Not that we are not to praise the Lord for all things, but we must first get our priorities right.

> *Then Eliphaz the Temanite answered and said, "If we assay to commune with thee, wilt thou be grieved? But who can withhold himself from speaking? Behold, thou hast instructed many, and thou hast strengthened the weak hands. Thy words have upholden him that was falling, and thou hast strengthened the feeble knees. But now it is come upon thee, and thou faintest; it toucheth thee, and thou art troubled." Is not this thy*

fear, thy confidence, thy hope, and the uprightness of thy ways?
(Job 4:1–6)

In this amazing portion of scripture found in Job 4:1–6, we see Job's friends laying a guilt trip on Job of sorts. Now though they are wrong most of the time they do make a good point here. So many times as believers we are uplifting and helping others. So many times we give them words of hope and peace to face their current situation, but how does it look when we face our own pain and yet we fall apart? Are we hypocrites and fools? As a pastor this is a very thin line that we walk as we are always trying to lift up our people with words of hope and Christ's power, but what happens when we are to face hard times? Are we going to crumble and in doing so what of our testimony and faith? I have sat alongside many hurting people, many weeping people, and I have given them words from the Bible and a word from my heart about the Lord's will and plan. They have found hope and strength in those words, but what happens when I am facing the same issues or problems, will I toss all of that wisdom out the window? Are God's words of comfort good for them but not for me? I hate it when people prove me wrong. I remember one particular time when I was all set to meet with a person from church to admonish them for errors on their part only to have them correct me. What was worse was the fact that they were right and I was wrong. Quickly I asked for forgiveness and confessed my error, and we both gave thanks to the Lord.

As we close out this chapter on light, glorious light of victory, I ask that you find in yourself a place to keep your praise. A place that is always ready to thank the Lord and see goodness in all that He does, even in the seemingly dark days. The day will come when this pain will pass and the light will shine on you like never before. The day when joy rules your heart as boldly as despair did when broken. The Lord does deliver and heal, and we know this to be true because He has given us the victor's crown. We are not losers in Christ but winners in Christ, and if Christianity was a place that always left us broken, sad, and bitter, then where would be the joy of the Lord to show off to the world? We must be victors because Christ is a victor, so let's get used to living that way and only expecting victorious things to happen. The world will take notice, and they will give glory to the Lord. Truly a candle placed under a bushel can't give off much light, and in fact it might just do more harm than good by putting the bushel ablaze. Let your light so shine before men that they may see your good works and glorify God in heaven. That's what it's all about—nothing more.

Never Forget the Pain

Our fathers understood not Thy wonders in Egypt;
they remembered not the multitude of Thy mercies; but
provoked Him at the sea, even at the Red Sea.

—Psalm 106:7

Those fixed on forgetting pain are destined to repeat it. I don't know where I heard that or if I just made it up, but regardless, it sure makes sense. As children we learn this lesson or at least we should: that if you play with something that bites back and it does, it will probably do it again. What does that mean to us? That lessons learned from pain need never be forgotten. In my life as a Christian I know this to be true, and I also know that I am a slow learner. I have, over the years, toyed with one sin or another, gotten burnt, and like a sheep to the slaughter I have headed right back into it again. One would think that being once bitten should make us twice shy, but it does not. The reason being is that sin tastes and looks so good that its pull is often stronger than our desire to please the Lord. If this were not so, then Adam and Eve would not have messed up either. With this thought in mind, let us also be careful that we do not make the same mistake and fall back into depression and anxiety by falling back into sin. To clarify this statement, let me say this. Though depression and anxiety are mighty tools in the Father's hand, tools that grow us for greatness for Him, they are also to some degree a result of sin. Many times in my life my failure to let go of certain sins and my failure to not heed the Lord's nudge to stop them left Him no choice but to zap me a bit with those old emotions. Not that He uses that on everyone, but on me it works real well. I get one single flick of those old pains and I am standing at attention to what the Lord is trying to say. I don't want to go back there, and if my sin leads me there, then I would be wise to stay far from that sin.

As we have shared throughout this book, depression and anxiety are actually blessed things if we learn what they are trying to teach us. Remember, the Lord doesn't just allow and introduce things into our lives to cause pain but to bring change and spirituality. If He did do it just to see us suffer, then He would be an awful tyrant and not the God of love that we know Him to be. It would be like being a parent and just punishing our child to his room just to see him suffer. No, a true parent doesn't enjoy punishment at all but hates the fact that they must implement it. As with the Lord it is the same, and if we would only learn the deeper truths that He is trying to show us, the less time maybe we would have to spend in that darkness. Sometimes I felt that I stayed so long in that darkness simply because I refused to submit to the Lord's will over my will. Reminds me of being a child at a certain age and my father back in the day struck me with his belt. In my apostasy I would arrogantly say, "That didn't hurt, so there." I really said that, and as I look back I see the same attitude that I have had toward God as an adult. "Lord, I like doing what I want, and though you punish me, I will not let it go, it is mine, all mine." Have you ever seen a very young child do that? When playing with a toy and other children want that toy and the child says, "Mine, mine, mine." Even if we slap their hand or try to pull it away, they only hold on more. Not to compare us to animals but my little beagle buddy does the same thing. When he has a toy or an object that is not his and I try to remove it, he will growl and fight me. Even if I give him a light tap on his nose, he will only squint his eyes but yet not let go. Amazing! Dear friend, as we close out this book with this last chapter, let us never, ever forget all the things we have learned and are learning through our emotional struggles. I would even suggest you write them down and go over them often so we don't repeat the mistake too quickly. Looking back on emotional trauma as in depression and anxiety leaves us with two choices in which to do it. We can look back with horror and fear and possibly throw ourselves back into it, or we can look back in awe as we see all that we have become through it. I have said it before and I will say it again, "I am so glad that time is passed, but I am also glad for that time." That is another reason why I feel the Lord keeps me on a short leash, so if I do wonder, He only needs to tug on me through those feelings and I am right back. I will not say it is easy to remember pain in a positive way, because certainly it is not, like trying to remember a tooth being pulled with joy and happiness. It is not going to happen in our own strength, but it can and must through the Lord's strength. In our Scripture today, we see the very familiar story of God's people Israel so quickly forgetting their pain and also great victory too quickly. "*Our fathers understood not Thy wonders in Egypt; they remembered not the multitude of Thy mercies; but provoked Him at the sea, even at the Red Sea*" (Psalm 106:7). Notice the word *provoked*. If we blatantly go straight away into a place where we have been clearly warned not to go, we risk the chance of provoking the Lord to anger. As a child constantly reaches for the cookie jar and waits for our eyes to see him, sooner or later that (good) parent will get up and scold that child. Now I don't want to keep pointing to depression and anxiety as punishments, nor do I think they are in most cases, but the fact remains that they can have that purpose. In my personal story I feel like 97 percent of the reason for what I had to endure was only due to the Lord working and molding me to be who I am and will become, but there is still that 3 percent that He did snap that whip and set me straight real fast from the error of my ways. No, I did not hate Him for it. Instead I was thankful that He loved me enough to care. Some sins were so strong that only a mighty force of correction could move me from them. Now that is the downside of remembering, but there is also the upside, which is all the vast wisdom, intimacy, and growth that we gained and are gaining through this blessed monster. In all of those years and moments I have walked so close with the Lord that in some regard I miss that one aspect of it. Hearing the Lord's will and feeling Him so intensely cannot be compared. The Lord speaks through emotional pain, and of that there can be no doubt. And if the Lord be speaking, then it must be good.

But What About Me? An Author's Confession

Now I am sure that in the back of your mind you are wondering how I turned out. What am I like now, and am I living in total victory and forever healed? Well, that is a fair question to ask and one most authors of such books as this would rather you not know. But being that I am not writing this book to be wealthy and make money off hurting people by selling them a lie so they buy it, it then leaves me with the freedom to be brutally honest with you because if I wasn't, then I would be in danger of lying to our Lord and only fooling myself. So with all that said, *as you know I'm a long talker,* here is where I am personally as of 2014. First, I stand by what I have said in this book. I stand by what has worked and not worked for me and all the people I have counseled. In many cases you will be healed in one way or another, but for some we might have to move on with one arm instead of two and simply learn how to live with what the Lord has chosen for us to possess. So as for me, I can gladly say that my depression has passed, not that I don't have down days, sad days, and days when I get discouraged, days when Satan beats me into submission with his lies until I stand up again and step back on his head. Now as to anxiety, well, I don't think it is possible to be a sinner by nature and never worry again. Of my anxiety, sure it pops up now and then, a panic attack here or there, but nothing that cripples me. When my bouts with anxiety set in, for the most part there is a trigger to them, but sometimes it is for no reason at all. It is as if a switch is flicked on in my brain and that tingle comes over me.

Mostly it passes, and at the worst it lasts a few days to a week. Yet my life today after all the storms of darkness is one filled with wonder, joy, blessings untold, laughing and living life the way the Lord intended. I am able to preach sermons with a passion like I never have before simply because of my life lessons from the valley of death. I counsel full-time as well as run a growing small country church, plus play with my Race Car Ministry (see NYT article on our webpage www.cbctruth.com) and Rusty Red Jeep Ministry (see rustyredjeep@gmail.com) with evangelization as my greatest purpose. I am under a lot of pressure, not to mention raising a family of three boys and loving a wife who deserves so much more after what I put her through. God has been good to me as He always has, and my future is filled with promises of great and wondrous things. But again that does not mean I will never face another bad day. Now the question I know you all want to know is one that most would never share or dare to even share, but to make this book as real and authentic as I possible can, I must, against my prideful nature, share this truth with you. Yes, I am still on medication, and until the Lord deems best for me to come off it, I must accept it as His will, as Paul had to accept the Lord's will of a thorn in the flesh for his life to keep him humble this also keeps me humble. My issue at the end of the day is rooted in my severe OCD, and probably ADHD, which led to my anxiety, which led to my massive depression. For over seventeen years now I have been off and on meds, hating being on them at every single moment. Yet every single time I tried to get off, I fall back into the darkness of anxiety attacks. Friends, I fear nothing, nor should I fear anything as a child of God, so in my case it is a chemical imbalance that is here to stay for now unless the Lord removes it, which He can. As I have stated it can be from environmental issues or the spirit of fear that Satan has left running rampant today or maybe all the recreational drugs that I took as a young person.

I played around with heavy psychotropic drugs as a youth, not to mention the loads of marijuana that I smoked among many other things. So who knows why or how, but it is what it is, and I must accept what my lot is if maybe to only show you that you are not a sub-Christian if you need to take medication. I take very little in that regard simply something to help with my OCD that seems to be the best for me and where I always fall back to. I take the lowest dosage there is, and it seems to take the edge off. Yes, I'm sure there will be many Christians who will say again that I simply need more faith, and maybe so, but also maybe like Jesus I need to accept the fate that the Father has ordained for me, to drink the bitter cup if that be His will. Yet in the end I have no hate for my medication anymore but thankfulness that the Lord found something for me that has allowed me to be myself again and live a normal and happy life for the most part. If anything it truly keeps me humble, and who knows, that might be the only reason for it. *"It is good for me that I have been afflicted; that I might learn Thy statutes"* (Psalm 119:71).

If You Care About Me, Read This Please

(For friends and family who don't
understand and want to help)
"Wherefore let him that thinketh he
standeth take heed lest he fall."

—1 Corinthians 10:12

I wasn't planning on having a thirteenth chapter, but I felt after looking over this completed book that I missed one very important point. The point that I speak of is this. What about our friends, family, loved ones, spouses, children, parents, and even coworkers? What about them, and what if there was a way that they could better understand what we are going through without expecting them to read an entire book? What if a simple chapter could clearly say what you always wanted to say to these well-meaning people, but just didn't have the right voice or vehicle to bring it to them? Well, today your wishes and prayers have been answered as this chapter is just for them. It is a chapter that will explain what you are going through, how it feels to be in that place, and most of all, what *they* can do to help you in your healing process. As I did in my book *Spiritual Living in a Sexual World* by writing a chapter just for the wives and loved ones of those dealing with the struggles with pornography and sexual addiction, so too I do the same for this monster of an issue. So that being said, I will begin to lay out some helpful guidelines for those who love us and care for us so that they can really help us in our healing instead of hurting us.

What Does It Feel Like to Be in Deep Depression and Living with Crippling Anxiety?

Sometimes the best way to describe something is to use an example that everyone else knows. Take burning your finger for a moment. Most people have and you know that a bad burn cannot be relieved but by sticking that finger in a glass of water. Yet it is hard to go to work with your finger in a glass of water. Now take that burning finger and take it out of the water and try to live. No one really sees the burn nor can feel it but you. No pain is as intense, and so it makes it hard if not impossible to think about anything else. So is that being selfish or just doing what the human body was designed by God to do? *The body focuses on that pain until that pain gets the attention it needs.* As to the intensity of depression and anxiety, the closest thing I have ever lived through that can come even close is the pain and suffering of food poisoning. Sure a stomach virus is pretty darn bad, but food poisoning is incomparable. I know this because I had it while on vacation. I spent three days in bed and in the bathroom while everyone else was out having fun. The fever, chills, nausea, and vomiting so badly that you cannot breathe. The desire to just want to feel better for a moment but you can't. The desire to just lie down and sleep and you can't. The waves of sickness that almost have you in tears. The need to be on the bowl and over the bowl at the same time and you can't. The desire to just be dead and even crying out to the Lord, "Just take me home right now." In that sickness nothing matters, not a new car, not an offer of money. All you can focus on is feeling better again and yet you doubt it will ever happen. For a day you actually think it will never go away. Now, dear friend, imagine feeling like that all the time, every day. Think you would start to get depressed? Think that just someone telling you to snap out of it and join the party could change it? Think also how frustrating it is when people are having fun and telling you to "just eat some crackers and you will be fine."

Now that is just a small idea of what living with depression and anxiety is like, yet there is so much more.

Remember when you were going for an important job interview where testing and hard questions would be asked. Remember how you felt, with the cold sweats the sweaty palms and the tumbling stomach. Remember having to go to court, or being called in by the IRS to audit your records. Remember waiting to have a tooth pulled and all the apprehension you felt. Now picture living with that all the time, every day, in every situation. Even while lying down at the beach on a wonderful summer day while everyone else is laughing and playing. This pain that we feel is unlike any other. People can't see it so people often find it hard to find sympathy for it. As a person who has suffered with this pain the greatest frustration is that people think you are faking or not really hurting. Imagine having two broken legs, one broken arm, and a dislocated shoulder. Now no one would expect you to go to work, drive, go shopping, and in fact they would feel great sorrow for you and offer to help. Yet imagine being that same person with all the broken bones and yet no one saw it but you. All they saw was a healthy-looking able-bodied person. Imagine the frustration of trying to get out of your car in agony, pain, and great immobility and yet no one saw the broken bones and casts. That is again how one feels when they suffer with emotional pain in a world that is blind to it. It is truly a silent pain, a silent scream. It is like being buried alive and pounding at the inside of the coffin yet no one hears you.

What You Can Do to Help

The Don'ts

Don't pretend to understand how they feel, but rather communicate how hard it is for you to comfort them when you don't know their pain.

Don't offer advice as if you were dealing with a bad cold or the flu. For the most part they have probably tried it all already.

Don't say things like "Just snap out of it, or you should be happy, you have so much going for you" or "If you had more faith, trusted in the Lord more, or would only want to get better, you would."

Don't be a judge when you haven't walked a mile in their shoes.

Don't tell that person that if they were a true Christian, they wouldn't need medication.

Don't tell them that if they only read their Bible more or went to your church, they would be all better.

Don't continually send e-mails, books, and devotionals about depression. They probably have a stack a mile high already. Instead ask them what they might like to read or hear.

Don't ever say dumb things like "All things work together for good." Not that it's not true, but sometimes there is a place and time for certain scriptures. In this book I do say those words but only in a tactful, practical, and gentle way.

Don't try to figure out for them what God is trying to do in their lives. If God needs to speak to them, He will convict their hearts at the proper time and place.

Don't say, "If you would just stop this sin or that, then the Lord would heal you."

Don't constantly ask them how they are feeling. People who are struggling and doing better don't like to be reminded about it and would rather enjoy the moment of feeling good.

Don't treat them like lepers. If you do take them out, then be yourself and don't treat them as if they have a major handicap. Remember that they want to be normal again and not be reminded of their pain.

Don't press them on anything If they really want to go out, they will let you know. This is a fine line though as sometimes they might need a little healthy prodding at times.

Don't let them get too far gone and know when it's time to call the family or even the police.

Don't treat them as if they are some mental patient who might go on a mass shooting spree. Yes, there are cases when this can happen, but you know your friend or loved one better than most. Most times unless there is some underling psychosis, they are just suffering from depression and anxiety.

Don't attack their faith and church if you happen to not be a believer as their faith might be the only thing that is holding them together. Instead praise them on how their faith means so much to them.

Don't get frustrated and impatient with them if a long period of time goes by and they are still struggling. More often than not depression and anxiety can last for years before it is brought under control.

Don't spread gossip or share what they tell you in confidence as you might be the only person they truly trust and you breaking that trust could be the one thing that pushes them over the edge.

Don't blame yourself for their failures and current situation as in most cases we tend to allow this pain to consume us, and though others might have hurt us, we still need to learn to live strongly in this world or decide to be beaten up by it.

The Dos

Do offer to pray for them and then really pray for them.

Do ask how you can help.

Do ask if they want visits or not.

Do let them know that the Lord works in many ways and maybe in time medication might be an option.

Do let them know that maybe seeing a Christian counselor might help and then do the legwork and get them the number of a good one.

Do offer to sit with them and ask if you could read the Bible or a devotional to them.

Do offer to help them out around the home but not too much help or they might depend on you instead of the Lord.

Do get stronger with your words if you see them sleeping too much and getting too much into a bad place. Use your words wisely here and say and do all things in prayerful love and consideration.

Do check on them if you haven't seen them in a while.

Do call them out of the blue to see how they are doing but don't overcall and check up on them.

Do look out for and report to their loved ones any unusual changes. Things like a sudden announcement that they are all better and everyone can stop checking on them. Sometimes this is the very first clue that suicide might be on their mind.

Watch out for changing in their eating, friends, and places they go to. Sometimes deep emotional pain can drive a person to become involved in unthinkable and often dangerous activities both psychically and spiritually.

Do praise them for hanging on and doing so much even with the pain they are facing.

Do try to change the subject if their complaining becomes persistent. True, some complaints must be taken into account, but obsessive complaining about life is not of God. Sometimes we might need to gently remind them of that.

Do say things like "I can't imagine what it's like to go through what you are going through and I won't pretend to know, but I do know that through God we can all beat anything."

Dear friends of hurting friends, never give up on your loved ones even if your patience grows thin. People suffering with depression and anxiety will go through many phases. Sometimes they will be irritable, impatient, nasty, bitter, and might even snap at you though you are trying your best. Even with those attacks don't give up on them. Try to remember by the examples that I gave what it might be like to be where they are. Try to put yourself in their place with a pain that no one sees. Try to understand that their pain and fears are just as real to them as cancer is to another. As for sympathy, it's another fine line. Give them some but not too much. Push them to keep fighting but not too much. Pray that the Lord would show you the right ways to help and not hurt. Be a willing sacrifice for them in regard to being beat up by the ones you love and are trying to help. Forgive them often and forget the nasty things they might say in their pain.

Be also ever leaning to hear the Lord's voice as when you feel that burden to call them. If you hear that still small voice even at three in the morning, then call them! It might be that the Lord is calling you to call them just at that time. And as our headline scripture reads,

Be careful that you don't take their pain too lightly as it might come upon you one day. I found out the hard way when dealing with people with emotional issues. I became very cold and questioning of their pains and lost my compassion for them quickly, never knowing that one day I would be in their shoes and worse. If we do not show compassion upon a loved one's pain we might be destined to experience it for ourselves. You may think that you are rock solid, on target with Christ, and that you could or would never fall into a depression or paralyzing anxiety, but you don't know that for sure. Be very careful in this regard.

In the next few portions of scriptures I have, we see some godly advice about another's pain and our response.

"But exhort one another daily, while it is called Today; lest any of you be hardened through the deceitfulness of sin" (Hebrews 3:13). Pride is a sin, and if our pride places us up above our suffering friends, well, we know what happens after a pride moment.

"For indeed he was sick nigh unto death: but God had mercy on him; and not on him only, but on me also, lest I should have sorrow upon sorrow" (Philippians 2:27). God's mercy on us is as sure as His mercy upon our loved ones. Don't ever look at your hurting friend as a lost cause at the same time you are trying to help them, for if you do, then you are a hypocrite and living a lie. Our friends, though in emotional pain, still have the ability to know that your words of comfort are empty. You can't tell someone all will be okay if you don't believe it.

"Brethren, if a man be overtaken in a fault, ye which are spiritual, restore such an one in the spirit of meekness; considering thyself, lest thou also be tempted" (Galatians 6:1). This scripture needs no explanation as it says clearly what we must know. If your loved one or friend is overtaken by emotional pains, be it from sin or simply as a tool of God to grow them, make sure your focus is on their healing, lest you fall into the same trap and pain.

"But I fear, lest by any means, as the serpent beguiled Eve through his subtlety, so your minds should be corrupted from the simplicity that is in Christ" (2 Corinthians 11:3). Be very careful in judging another's pain. Be very careful in praising yourself for living a great Christian life in your own eyes. Satan looks for such pride and might just hang you by the very rope you think is your life line. Watch out for the tempters snare.

"But I keep under my body, and bring it into subjection: lest that by any means, when I have preached to others, I myself should be a castaway" (1 Corinthian 9:27). As to our own lives we should always be walking circumspectly and making sure our emotional ship is in order. The mind is a complicated machine, and if we are not quick to maintain it, it can quickly fall apart. Don't be so quick to preach to your suffering loved one about holiness, faith, and trusting in God when you are not doing the same. Remember to look in your mirror daily before you tell people what's in theirs. You might be closer to falling into depression and anxiety than you think, and the old phrase "There for the grace of God goes I" might be more relevant than you think.

On another note lest we judge too quickly our fallen and broken brethren, let's not forget the words of the great apostle Paul. In 1 Corinthians 2:1–5 we notice that even though Paul was blessed with a massive dose of the Holy Spirit, it didn't leave him in a state of happy, happy, joy, joy all day long. Notice how Paul lived at times especially during trials. Notice that it wasn't always a peace-filled joyride of hand-waving praise and worship sessions. Notice how sometimes the fear, trembling, and weakness remained. Notice that being in Christ doesn't always mean being in a state of constant smiles and laughter. Notice that Paul was just like you and me, a man faced with great trials in Christ's service, yet a man who also worried. Notice the words "I was with you," meaning that he understood their fears and trials because he went through his own. Dear friend of a friend, remember that being in Christ doesn't mean that anxiety is gone forever or somehow makes you a lesser Christian. Be very slow to judge another as we might have to face the same pain one day to squelch our condescending attitude and tongue.

> *And I, brethren, when I came to you, came not with excellency of speech or of wisdom, declaring unto you the testimony of God. For I determined not to know any thing among you, save Jesus Christ, and him crucified. And I was with you in weakness, and in fear, and in much trembling. And my speech and my preaching was not with enticing words of man's wisdom, but in demonstration of the Spirit and of power:*

> *That your faith should not stand in the wisdom of men, but in the power of God.* (1 Corinthians 2:1–5)

In closing, remember again that emotional pain is just as real and painful as physical pain, and sometimes it's even worse. Don't make light of a dear one who is in its clutches. Show love, compassion, and great spiritual maturity. The Lord might be using their pain to actually work on you. Maybe your loved one's hurt is only a test to see how you respond to it. Think about how Jesus would handle a hurting broken soul. Ask questions. Find out their history and why they might have fallen into this dark place. The eyes of the Lord might just be upon you just as they are on your dear hurting friend.

> *But take heed lest by any means this liberty of yours become a stumbling block to them that are weak.* (1 Corinthians 8:9)

Pastors and Leaders in Ministry, *It Can Happen to You Too*

Just when I thought I was finished with this book, I had a *Columbo* moment. You know the TV detective who would always say, "Just one more thing?" Well, this is my "just one more thing." I read an article in the news that really motivated me to say just one more thing on this subject. That is, depression, anxiety, and mental illness can affect those in leadership too. In fact what better place for the enemy to pin point his attacks but at the leadership. If He can take us down and out, then He can take out a whole congregation with one swipe at its head. More and more I am seeing this in my own ministry. Be it my elders, deacons, worship leaders, and everyone else in ministry leadership. It appears that their families and personal lives are under more and more attack. I have seen it in depression in one of my elders and in a few of my deacons. Anxiety and fear seems to follow them through out their day and into their home so heavily that they get so consumed with their own pains that they cannot focus on the ministry of the church, which in turn places more pressure on me, the pastor, and the next thing you know the captain of the ship can no longer pilot it. I have had people in ministry head positions call me in a frantic pitch, "Pastor, please come, I'm having a panic attack and I can't move, I'm frozen." Dear friends, this is spreading like wildfire, and the enemy knows it as he is the one personally fanning the flames. Even people in the secular psychiatric field are falling prey to this as doctors and health care providers themselves are increasingly on medication due to the overwhelming amount of people in emotional free falls. My own dear friend who runs a Christian counseling center ended up bed bound and ultimately on medication. Oh, this is no chance occurrence but a carefully planned attack. Remember Satan walks about as a roaring lion seeking whom He may devour and those who He seems to be seeking most is those in ministry head positions. Following is an article written by Jennifer LeClaire who is a news editor at Charisma magazine. She points out some interesting facts to consider and if anything keeps us on our toes as the magnified pressures of ministry as this current age seeks to roll us down.

[In another church tragedy, Pastor Isaac Hunter—the son of the spiritual adviser to President Obama—has reportedly taken his own life. Hunter's death is making national headlines because of his megachurch father Pastor Joel Hunter's influence on the White House, his marriage troubles and an undated suicide note found last year, but his death is far from the only pastoral suicide in recent months. Just days ago, a pastor who was grieving his dead wife reportedly shot himself in front of his mother and son, expressing that he was hearing his dead spouse's voice and footsteps. Pastor Ed Montgomery and his late wife, prophetess Jackie Montgomery, served at the Full Gospel Assemblies International church in Hazel Crest, Ill. In November, a Georgia pastor killed himself in between Sunday services. Larrinecia Sims Parker, wife of the Rev. Teddy Parker Jr., found the pastor in the driveway of their home with a self-inflicted gunshot wound, Houston County coroner Danny Galpin reports.

Why the sudden rash of pastors committing suicide? Suicide is not a new problem among clergy, but three known suicides in less than two months begs a deeper look at the issue.

There is no lack of statistics about pastors and depression, burnout, health, low pay, spirituality, relationships and longevity—and none of them are good. According to the Schaeffer Institute, 70 percent of pastors constantly fight depression, and 71 percent are burned out. Meanwhile, 72 percent of pastors say they only study the Bible when they are preparing for sermons; 80 percent believe pastoral ministry has negatively affected their families; and 70 percent say they don't have a close friend.

The Schaeffer Institute also reports that 80 percent of seminary and Bible school graduates will leave the ministry within five years. It's not clear how many commit suicide, but it is clear that pastors are not immune to it. Psychologists point to several reasons why people commit suicide, from depression to psychosis to stressful life situations. But one thing is certain: Whatever drives someone to take their own life ultimately begins in the mind. Suicidal thoughts precede suicide.

"Suicidal thoughts have numerous causes," according to Mayo Clinic. "Most often, suicidal thoughts are the result of feeling like you can't cope when you're faced with what seems to be an overwhelming life situation. If you don't have hope for the future, you may mistakenly think suicide is a solution. You may experience a sort of tunnel vision, where in the middle of a crisis you believe suicide is the only way out."

As it turns out, suicidal thoughts are not uncommon. Nearly 8.3 million adults age 18 and older in the United States—that's 3.7 percent—had serious thoughts of suicide in the past year, according to a study called "Suicidal Thoughts and Behaviors Among Adults > 18 Years" released by the Centers for Disease Control and Prevention. Although some suicides are impulsive, most are planned out. More than 2 million adult Americans made a suicide plan in the past year, and about half that many went through with the plan.

Again, suicide starts with a thought. Indeed, every action we take starts with a thought. As one who struggled with depression for years, I am not trying to oversimplify the solution, but rather merely point out one contributing factor. Many of the harmful actions we take originate from the seed of a thought Satan whispers to our souls. That seed grows as our minds reason out the benefits of acting on the thought. For those contemplating suicide, I believe the seed grows in their minds as they reason themselves out of living because life's circumstances are too overwhelming.

When the enemy plants a vain imagination in our minds, we have two choices: cast it down or meditate on it. When we meditate on vain imaginations, we tend to connect demonic dots that create skewed pictures of reality. Believing what we see in our thought life is real, we talk ourselves into taking action based on a wrong perception. Although there are issues of chemical imbalances, I believe this is what happens with many suicides. The enemy plants a seed in the form of a thought that an already distraught soul doesn't discern as a demonic attack on their life.

If we want to win the battle against suicide in the pulpit and the pew, we need to, among many other things, take hold of Scriptures that instruct us about the battle in our mind. Paul told us, "The weapons of our warfare are not carnal but mighty in God for pulling down strongholds, casting down arguments and every high thing that exalts itself against the knowledge of God, bringing every thought into captivity to the obedience of Christ, and being ready to punish all disobedience when your obedience is fulfilled" (2 Cor. 10:4–6). No one can take your thoughts captive for you, but you can take your own thoughts captive, and it starts with girding up the loins of your mind (1 Pet. 1:13).

Paul also offered this advice: "Whatever things are true, whatever things are noble, whatever things are just, whatever things are pure, whatever things are lovely, whatever things are of good report, if there is any virtue and if there is anything praiseworthy—meditate on these things. The things which you learned and received and heard and saw in me, these do, and the God of peace will be with you" (Philippians 4:8–9). If we do what the Word says—if we meditate on what the Word tells us to meditate on—the enemy's seeds won't take root in our souls.

If you see your pastor or anyone else struggling with depression or hear them speak disturbing thoughts that aren't in line with the Word of God, pray and ask God what He would have you do. Then do it. Suicide is a leading cause of death in the United States, and the enemy is targeting our spiritual leaders in this hour. Let's rise up and battle against this disturbing trend in the name of Jesus]

Jennifer LeClaire is news editor at Charisma. She is also the author of several books, including The Spiritual Warrior's Guide to Defeating Jezebel. You can e-mail Jennifer at jennifer.leclaire@charismamedia.com or visit her website. You can also join Jennifer on Facebook or follow her on Twitter.

Thank you, Jennifer, for this amazing profound article and thank you for allowing me to include it in this book. I know it is of the Lord as I was just ready to put down my pen on this project when I read this. So in closing out this bonus, bonus chapter let us remember that no one is immune and you are not alone. Don't always assume everyone else's life is peaches and cream simply because you see them smiling on Sunday mornings. I remember this one older gentleman who began attending my church and searching for God's truth in the process. One day he came up to me after a sermon and said, "Pastor Scott, I want to be like you, so full of joy and passion and peace." I immediately shot back at him and said, "Oh, dear friend, you are very misled. I am just like you with fears, problems, and days when I just want to give up the fight. No, what you see up at the pulpit is the Lord holding me up by the boot straps. Without Him I am Jell-O and nothing more but a man with a nice suit." In fact the truth be told to all reading this book, I can't even walk without Jesus holding my hand. I am weak and undone, and apart from the Holy Spirit's indwelling presence, I would not even be able to continue another day. Now some might say that that's a sign of weakness, but to me it's a sign of strength for the man who knows he is nothing without Christ. He is a man who the Lord can take to the highest mountain peak. May we all be that man or woman for Christ and always remembering that *but for the grace of God, go I.* Please pray for your pastors and leaders. Pray for their families and Children as this day and age of the church, the enemy knows time is not His friend, and so He has turned up the heat of despair and despondency all the way up to ten.

Now as we close this book out, I also want you to consider where you go from here. First, if you have not purchased my companion devotional called *Depression, Anxiety and the Child of God– The Devotional*, please do so to help you daily through this battle. Second, if it be that you are still in the pain or beginning to come out of it, you must remember this–your pain was never about you but about you growing and others benefiting from it, and that is why I suggest a few of the following things. Get involved in your church and find out how you can share what you have learned and are learning. If your church is silent on this issue, then make sure that it does not stay that way. Form a support group and or find out who else is hurting this way. You will be surprised at how many are. A good way to get people to come forward is to take an anonymous poll via them filling out a questionnaire without their names. In your prayer life constantly ask the Lord to bring you people who are suffering with the same thing. He will, and as soon as you start ministering to others in need, you will see how quickly your need falls away. If you are a computer person, start a Christian's blog or forum for those who suffer with emotional issues. Check out my blog, depressionanxietygod.blogspot.com. Also, serve, serve, serve, is all I can say, because the quicker you make this about the Lord and others, the quicker it stops being about you. Now certainly if you are still at the very dark, heavy stages of this trip, then you can hold off on helping others until you are ready, but don't wait too long. I remember after having my first surgery, the first thing the doctors did was get me up and walking. I thought I should rest and heal a bit longer, but they said, "No, the sooner you get up and walking, the sooner you will be heading home and healing." As to this book, I pray that you would share it with others and also feel free to contact me personally at my Web page or through my special e-mail. I will try to stay in contact with as many of you as I can. As we speak I am planning on many different things as the Lord deems proper and expedient. As for now, please friend our Facebook page, visit our Web page to leave a comment about your struggle and this book, either pro or con. Also look for dates of our US speaking engagements tour. Ask your church if they are interested in having me come and speak on these topics as well as speaking about my first book *Spiritual Living in a Sexual World*, a book about and for Christian men struggling with pornography and sexual addiction. I would love to meet you all, and through our combined stories, we can lead many to victory in Christ. I look forward to hearing your victory story.

For questions about *Depression, Anxiety, and the Child of God* and bookings for speaking engagements contact Pastor Scott at depressionanxietygod@gmail.com

For questions about *Spiritual Living in a Sexual World* and bookings for speaking engagements regarding porn addiction and sexual dysfunctions in the life of Christian men and its effects on their families, contact Pastor Scott at spirituallivinginasexualworld@gmail.com

In Christ,
Pastor S. R. Kraniak, Th.B. -MMCC

Closing Thought

Okay, you read the book, but don't stop there. I pray that you will pick up the devotional companion book for daily thoughts throughout each coming year. Some things you might not have agreed upon, and some maybe you have. Dear friend and fellow sufferer, I didn't write this book because I wanted to, but because I went through what you're going through, and I knew there had to be purpose. The purpose I felt was that through my pain and gain, others would find peace also. Will this book cure all your ills, keep you smiling from ear to ear each and every day? No. If it did, then it would be conflicting with the Bible because the Lord never promised us that here anyway. Life is hard, but God is good. If you can at least come away from this book with that understanding, I would be most happy. To know that you learned to be blessed or at least found blessings through your depression and anxiety, again that would make me most joyful. A. W. Tozer once wrote, "Sometimes God has to keep away encouraging results so we can learn to trust Him without them." I know that is hard and I know, dear Lord, I know how rotten depression and anxiety can feel, but I also know what God can do through these pains. Please learn to thank the Lord for what He is allowing you to suffer through. Look for the lessons He is trying to teach. And most of all, get excited about the special blessing of getting to know Christ closer then most. Yes, I truly believe that these times of depression and anxiety truly bring us where no man has gone before. Totally alone with our thoughts and totally alone with Christ. If we are to ever see Him in this life, you won't get any closer than through the blessed gift of emotional pain.

Disclaimers and Explanations

Throughout this book you will come across my own vernacular and poetic license. Because of this I want to put together a short list of terms and phrases that you will see and what I am trying to express by them. I will also use psychological terms as well as biblical terms that I have modified and created if you will, *hybrids of these terms*. I do this not because I simply want to be bombastic or that I am above the mental health community or theological community but simply because I feel it better helps to explain what I have learned through real life (rubber meets the road) existence.

The wonderful blessing of depression

A wonderful tool in the Master's hand

I write these because I do see depression not as a monster always from Satan but at times a wonderful and very effective tool for God getting our attention.

My personal depression has been the catalyst to major work-ings and movements in my life. At the end of the day they were the best thing that ever happened to me.

Fellow Sufferer

I use this term throughout the book because I am a sufferer like you. I have suffered with depression and anxiety, and I have been in remission, but I do not know if I will ever be totally cured. But maybe that is a good thing, for as I have stated over and over again, no man can walk closer with Christ than when he walks in the robe of emotional distress. It is good!

The Word of God

I always capitalize the word *word* when referring to the Word of God. Jesus is the living Word not just a word.

A child of God by faith in Jesus Christ

I always say this when speaking about a true Christian, as the Bible is clear that we are only children of God through faith in Jesus Christ and no other way.

—Galatians 3:26

When referring to God or Jesus, I will always use the capital *H* in *He* to signify God or Christ as opposed to just anyone.

Mental illness

Any form of emotional issues from spiritual to psychological. To separate them sometimes is very hard as the two are so very bound together by diverse yet similar counterparts yet. Not all emotional trauma is mental illness, and not all mental illness is simple emotional trauma.

Most Christians that suffer with depression and anxiety do not have mental illness but may have some of the similar characteristics of it. Many treatments are the same for both.

Mental illness has a great stigma that comes along with it, and most people find it easier to say they are suffering with a slight anxiety issue than to say they are suffering from mental illness. Let us always use care and caution before we throw these types of terms around.

Depression

- Seasonal
  The mild blues we encounter during the change of seasons, like autumn, Christmas, mid winter, rain, and overcast weather.

- Situational
  You lose your job and you are sad and depressed (normal depression).

- Clinical / severe
  Lack of motivation, lack of will to live, suicidal thoughts, bedridden, lack of appetite, or increase of appetite (most likely requires medication).

- Mild /moderate
  The beginning stages of more severe depression but not in every case.

- Geographical
  Living in a colder, wetter, cloudier area, also in an economically deprived location.

- General /daily life
  Having to go to work when you don't feel like it, your raise at work never came. Have a cold and not feeling well, just having a bad day.

Anxiety

- Severe anxiety

  This is crippling anxiety where ability to function at work or even at home has been compromised: loss of appetite, increase of appetite, weight loss, stomach issues, cold/hot sweats, shortness of breath, feeling of being frozen and not being able to move, numbness and tingling sensations in arms, in legs, feet, and or hands. Sweaty palms, chest pains, desire to flee and lie down (most likely requires medication).

- Moderate anxiety

  Same as above yet with being able to function (functional). Uncomfortable in crowds of people.

- Panic Attack–See *Anxiety attack*

- Anxiety Attack -

  Massive overwhelming blast of anxiety. Normally comes with no warning. Comes with a great desire to flee and move to an open location. Vomiting can accompany this, and *heart attack*–like symptoms. Chest pains. The person usually demands they go to the hospital and then after many tests nothing is found

- Fear

  What God has placed in us to keep us alive; fear of being in a lion's den is normal fear.

- Anxiety disorder

  Constant state of mild anxiety and or panic attacks.

- Life anxiety

  Going for a new job, meeting a new person—these are normal anxieties.

Worrying about a coming storm, or when the phone rings at 3:00 a.m.

- Situational anxiety

  Similar to life anxiety but more focused on real high pressure situations—as in having to sing the "Star-Spangled Banner" at a major event in front of many people, fear of failure or major decision making, buying a new home or car, investing large amounts of your money.

- Spiritual anxiety

  Anxiety that comes after we sin, and know we have disappointed the Lord. If you don't get this anxiety, then you should be concerned.

Suicide

- Cognitive – To think about taking your life when depression has set in is not uncommon and in most cases is normal. These thoughts can come and go and wishing that a simple escape might help is again normal. Many people think about taking their lives at times, but it never goes further than it being a passing thought. The thought of just being so tired you wouldn't care if a big truck ran you down. Now what is a concern is when that thought crosses the line as we will see in *operational* suicide.
- Operational – To plan out, set up, put together the components needed to make it happen. Writing it out on paper, looking for a location. Fixating on it day and night. These are very dangerous warning signs, and they should be shared with someone you trust as soon as possible. In these cases around the clock supervision is needed.

Note: Throughout this book I will refer to all types of anxiety and depression. Sometimes I will not signify which one I am speaking about. When this happens, it means that the same advice is then to be used in all cases of said depression or anxiety with the possible omission or addition of medications.

Finale note: This book and companion devotional book (purchased separately) is based upon the studies and experience of S. R. Kraniak. They are his opinions, which he has found to be successful in most but not all situation and peoples. If you are suffering from depression and or anxiety, Pastor Scott recommends that you see your mental health care provider as soon as possible. Taking medications or not taking them is a very critical decision and should only be decided upon after your doctor has given you those instructions. If you are thinking about taking your life, even in the mildest form, please also see your local health care provider or call your local 911. Any people referred to in this book are actual people that I have counseled, but their names have been changed to protect their privacy.

Also, the views expressed here by Pastor Scott Kraniak are not necessarily the views of the Centereach Bible Church www.cbctruth.com

Pastor Scott Kraniak also emphatically states that his conclusions are based on his years of study, counseling, and personal experiences, yet that does not mean that his ideas and techniques are clinically proven or can be viewed as a form of treatment. This book is a book of suggestions, not a cure for such or any conditions, and should be digested in that manner. Pastor Scott Kraniak takes no responsibility for the outcome of anyone's personal mental condition.

About the Author

S. R. Kraniak is the pastor of the *Centereach Bible Church*, a small church in Long Island, New York (www.cbctruth.com). He has been pastor there since 2006. Before that, he was pastor of a small church in Green Valley, California, *Green Valley Bible Chapel*. While in California, Pastor Scott ran a counseling and youth ministry while running the little chapel in a bi-vocation status. He also authored a newspaper column called *Ask Pastor Scott*, a write-in Christian help column. After moving back to New York where he is originally from, he took over the *Centereach Bible Church*, which is also the church he came to know Christ through way back in 1983 and in 1985 he began attending. Back at the CBC he continued his Christian counseling practice, which he had been doing back as far as 1990 on his own. He also had a live call-in radio show known as *The Last Call Radio Show*, another counseling-based call-in show. The show aired on two different local radio stations for about two years. Pastor Scott also wrote in a local newspaper column on Long Island called *Ask the Clergy*. Pastor Scott was also a frequent guest on a local radio show called *Iron sharpens Iron*, plus a part of the *Pastors' Round Table* show on that same station. For a while Pastor Scott tried his hands at getting into local government where he chaired the local town youth board, was a board member of two local civic based boards, and was outspoken at many town board meetings in regard to youth-oriented issues. Back at CBC he also ran a youth-oriented coffee house and numerous youth programs.

Pastor Scott also authored/published a book called *Spiritual living in a Sexual World* (AuthorHouse 0987087), a book about and for Christian men struggling with pornography and sexual addictions. In regard to that book, he did seminar speaking about that issue at local churches, and Christian-based venues and also on local radio shows. Currently Pastor Scott is the *Track Chaplain* of a local race track where he ministers the Gospel there to race car drivers and hot rod enthusiasts through a ministry called *Racing with Jesus Ministries (RWJM.COM)*, see *NY Times* 9/2013 article. Today in regard to his counseling practice he specializes in depression, anxiety, sexual addictions, teen cutting, and family counseling. He has a master's degree in Christian counseling and a bachelor's degree in theology. He is also a member of the New York State Mental Health Counselors Association, and a member of a local ministers association called Suffolk County Evangelical Ministers Fellowship. Yet with all of that, things have not always been easy or smooth-sailing. In 1997 he encountered his first bout with anxiety and depression, which was so serious that he almost took his life. Also extreme OCD haunted him, and sometime later he would slip again into depression and anxiety. It was not something he ever expected but something that he knew he had to deal with. It was either give up or dig in and fight. Even till this day there are times where those feelings pop up to remind him how trusting in Jesus Christ and having deep intimacy with Him is the only hope in a world with much pain and suffering. He began seeing his calling in this area and began being an outspoken advocate for discussion on topics of depression and anxiety in the church through seminar speaking on the issues and joining a local Christian mental health care providers group. Pastor Scott is fifty-one years old as of this writing, and married for over twenty-six years to his best friend Julie. They have three boys—Jacob, Aaron and their youngest Luke, which were all homeschooled. Pastor Scott, besides serving Jesus Christ and being a part of the hot rod ministry, also enjoys old Jeeps, which he mentions often in this book. His dream is to be able to travel the country and speak on depression and anxiety in the church today. Some might not like his hard-nosed approach to life, his way of treating depression and anxiety, his Gospel presentation, and doing what's right, but that's just how he is. Old-school preaching without being afraid to talk about sin and God's justice as well as his love. His favorite authors are A. W. Tozer, Watchmen Nee, Dietrich Bonhoffer, David Wilkerson, and Ray Comfort, plus many, many more old-school preachers. Pastor Scott was raised a Roman Catholic, turned atheist, dabbled a short time in the occult, and even played drums in the heavy metal music scene of the 1980s before coming to know Jesus Christ as Lord. If you would like to have Pastor Scott speak at your church, please contact him at depressionanxietygod@ gmail.com or on Facebook.

About the Book

Depression, Anxiety, and the Child of God is a book that has been long overdue. It is a book that takes the taboo out of being a Christian and suffering with emotional issues. All throughout the Bible we see accounts of great people of God being afraid, depressed, panicking, even thinking suicidal thoughts. If the Bible speaks about these issues, why don't we? Far too long the church has been silent and lacking the education to deal with these things. Yet the bigger question is, why is all of this happening? When did depression and anxiety become so common in a world with so much? Today is a brave new world with new challenges that pastors and clergy from days gone by never had to deal with—the dismantling of the family unit, pornography, a sexually permissive, anti-biblical and anti-moral society. The church has lost all if its significance and effectiveness. In a recent poll of the least respected jobs in the world, being a pastor was at the top of the list, above even a used car salesman. The church has no clout or relevance today, and that's only because we have let ourselves get mired in foolish fights while letting the important ones fall to the wayside. To the world today we are a laughingstock, known only by our hatred of certain select peoples and pet peeve sins. Why aren't we known for Christ's love, His redemption available to all, and Christ's high standard of moral excellence? No, we have become like the world, and with it we have acquired the world's problems including problems like depression and anxiety. Instead we got too focused on political issues and minor doctrinal issues that only divide the church instead of bringing it together. These all began the weakening of the peoples. Worship vs. hymns, arms up vs. arms down in worship, pews or chairs—we have made the church into a race to see who can fill theirs faster than the next guy, and we will use any means to achieve that goal. We have focused so much on the worship experience with light shows and multiscreen sanctuaries that our church buildings look more like concert halls and nightclubs than a place to learn of Christ. These all began the weakening of the peoples. We have forgotten foundational truths that hold the church up—things like Christ's blood, the cross, judgment, redemption, sacrifice, service, evangelism and seeking the lost. These all began the weakening of the peoples. Instead we have focused on making people feel good, which you cannot do if Christ is not preached first, and yes, even preaching the hard stuff like hell and judgment. Without understanding what we were saved from, the preaching of God's love alone loses all significance. These all began the weakening of the peoples. We have forgotten to equip our people with the answers so they can debate the world with knowledge—wisdom about creation, the young Earth, Christ's return and the hope of it, the love for Israel and being willing to fight for the Gospel above our own gospel. Instead we have placed our hope in today, fun, and what I am going to get out of this. These all began the weakening of the peoples. This book tosses out all the wasted effort in church building today and attempts to place God's people back on the right track to glorifying Him and not self, by seeking to build God's kingdom, not simply to build our own. It is through these simple steps that emotional stability can be established again. Depression can be neutralized, anxiety destroyed. See, if we attempt to find happiness in this world and the things of it, we are setting ourselves up for a fall. This world can never bring happiness, so we should not attempt to find it here. People are depressed and anxious today because they see the troubles of this world and yet are only taught about the prosperity that is promised in Christ. Soon they wake up and realize they have been sold a lie. They waited for a rose-garden life when Christ only promised them a thorn-garden life here, and the result is despondency. The only promise of perfection we have promised is yet to come in eternity. It is not that the Gospel has failed or the church has failed but that we changed what the Gospel and church were supposed to be teaching. That is, *in this world you shall have tribulation*. Get used to it and find your peace in Christ. Not in money, health, new cars, big homes, fun party times. Those things are certainly not for certain, and so when they don't happen, we fall. But instead of blaming the false teachers out there, we blame the Lord and conclude that God has failed us, and in time we will begin to even think that God doesn't even exist at all. These all began the weakening of the peoples. Once you cross that line, then there is no hope, joy, help, or promises. You are then truly alone in a self-imposed hell made with human hands. What else can follow but the emptying of the churches, the darkening of the soul, and a search for an escape from our pain through everything but Christ. Drugs, sex, self-serving, and suicide become the way out. This book attempts to turn all of that on its side just as Christ turned this world upside down. We are due for a flip, and Pastor Scott hopes to make that flip back to true Christianity through his life's work put into this book.

Note-
This is the first part of this work on depression and anxiety
Make sure to get the companion book called
Depression, Anxiety, and the Child of God the
(Twelve-Month Devotional)

Personal note pages

Personal note pages

CPSIA information can be obtained
at www.ICGtesting.com
Printed in the USA
FFOW03n1746030617
36237FF